The Blue Nib Magazine 35
New Poetry, Fiction & Essays

September 15th 2018

Edited by Shirley Bell

The Blue Nib Magazine 35
New Poetry, Fiction & Essays

September 15th 2018

First published in Great Britain in 2018 by The Blue Nib

Every effort has been made to reflect each author's intention re the format and content
of the piece, however the default style, which has been applied,
is Times New Roman 12, single-spaced

ISBN: 978-1-9999550-5-2

Contents

New Fiction   **68**

Reviews   **98**

New Essays   **119**

Segments   **133**

Biographies of Contributors   **140**

Editorial

A huge welcome to this, the first print issue of The Blue Nib. Dave Kavanagh and I feel that the magazine has come a very long way in a little over a year and we are very excited to be moving into this format, alongside our continuing e-zine presence at thebluenib.com.

Jane Simmons, our new Reviews Editor, writes about Denise Riley's *Say Something Back* and Carolyn Jess-Cooke's *Boom!* We also welcome a new member of the review team, Emma Lee, who is bringing an enormous amount to the magazine. In this issue she has reviewed *The Becoming of Lady Flambé* by Holly Magill, and she has also contributed poetry and has written about her role as co-editor of *Over Land, Over Sea: poems for those seeking refuge.* These diverse contributions really demonstrate Emma's varied talents. Her biographical poetry is so effective at conjuring personalities and situation and bringing Ella Fitzgerald back to life.

I have also featured L. Shapley Bassen's review of *Arcadia* by Iain Pears while Simran Keshwani looks at issues of privacy and surveillance in her review of the movie *Snowden.* In essays, Nigel Jarrett looks at memory and its vagaries in *Forgetting to Remember,* Samantha Maw looks back on her experiences as a teacher in Uganda, and Aurora M. Lewis writes of the discrimination she has experienced throughout her life in her engrossing account, *A Black California Baby-Boomer.*

Now to poetry. What a joy it is to have so much room for these exciting poets. I have to say at this point that I have many fine contributions in waiting - submissions to the site and emailed submissions. Please be patient. I do read absolutely everything with close attention, so do be assured that your work is not forgotten! If you have made multiple submissions to other sites as well as The Blue Nib (which is obviously tempting though not altogether welcome), please do let me know if works have been taken! It is so discouraging to select an exciting batch of poems and to find that they have been taken for publication elsewhere, and it also consumes time and disrupts my plans for the issue.

So what about the poets I have chosen? Anne Walsh Donnelly, our Chapbook 2 winner, has submitted poems that have an engaging conversational tone and lots of energy. I am especially proud that The Blue Nib was the first magazine ever to publish any of Anne's poems. (And see also Anne's fine story in this issue). Tom Paine is a sharp and observant poet, with wide ranging subject choices and compelling narratives. As well as her fine review, L. Shapley Bassen has contributed poetry. Like Tom Paine she is also good at concise observations, written in a succinct and elegant style. Cathy Donelan has sent some delightful subtle and delicate poetry.

I am particularly pleased to showcase Nora Cornell's work. Her poems are surprisingly mature for a high school student (she assures me that I am not being patronising). Her poems are so perceptive and thought-provoking.

Re: Individual poems – regular readers will know that I always like to have a bit of a pick'n'mix of stand-alone work. Sometimes a set of poems doesn't make the cut, but there is often one that stands out. Sometimes a poem is quirky, or maybe I choose a dialect poem which is interesting because it honours dialects. D. J. Tyrer's two short poems are acidic and amusing. Sunil Sharma gives us a frenetic Mumbai and what can I say about Arthur Broomfield's surrealist poetry? A thought provoking and simultaneously completely baffling stream of consciousness that comes meditatively. I chose this one because there was enough cat imagery woven through it to appeal to my sense of order in the midst of chaos!

Michael A. Griffith's precise and poignant poetry is always a delight and we are thrilled that his chapbook, to be published by The Blue Nib, will soon be available.

Jeremy Nathan Mark's passionate *You can take my water* sits alongside his biting criticism of racism in *Time pieces* which begs to be read alongside *A Black California Baby-Boomer* by Aurora M. Lewis.

Marissa McNamara's poignant yet clear-eyed poems sit alongside Polly Richardson (Munnelly) 's passionate work. Nathan Fidler has sent sensitive and observant poetry and Roy Liran's work is concise, thoughtful and full of ideas. We are also looking forward to publishing his chapbook in the near future.

And finally, two unusual poets. Charles G. Lauder: I like the way he nails each piece, whatever the scale, and I was fascinated by the inexorable 'rise' of Kaplan. Stephen House: I enjoyed the overwhelming rush of these frenetic poems, and their edgy subject matter, dealing with sex, a lost father, addiction, anger and despair.

The next print issue is out on December 15th 2018 please send submissions by the end of November at the very latest.

Shirley Bell, Poetry Editor & Editor in Chief

I am excited and honoured to be the new Fiction Editor for The Blue Nib. I'm delighted to be taking on the role as the magazine launches in print, as well as online, after 34 successful editions as an e-zine. I'm London-based and disappointed that I won't be there for the much-anticipated launch event in Dublin. As regular readers will know, so far, the e-zine has focused primarily on poetry. The decision to include short fiction demonstrates the magazine's ever-increasing popularity and the high quality of the work submitted to date. I'm very attached to print media, and I enjoy reading a physical object. Reading content online we are sometimes inclined to skim. Print has that appealing physicality and encourages us to slow down and savour what we're reading.

It is the perfect time to begin to include short fiction, which is having something of a resurgence. The viral phenomenon *Cat Person* by US writer Kristen Roupenian was unexpectedly one of the New Yorker's most read pieces of 2017. It was subsequently snapped up by the Penguin Random House imprint Jonathan Cape, and has been published as a stand-alone work of short fiction this year. Somewhat less contemporaneously, in the 1800s Edgar Allan Poe (now underrated, but then a prominent literary critic) was a fan of short fiction. Poe felt that it was one of the literary forms in which "genius" was best demonstrated. (In his view, it was second only to rhyming poetry. You may or may not agree with that!)

Short-form fiction, designed to be read in a single sitting, demands full artistic control. Many writers feel that mastery of the short form is even more difficult than the craft of novel-writing. In a piece of short fiction, every word must earn its place. In contrast, the novel is permitted the luxury of digression and expansive character studies. Of course, it also has to engage the attention for that much longer.

The writer Paul McVeigh used the analogy of the composition of a photograph versus making a full-length film. Both take skill and observation, but their aims differ. A character sketch, a snapshot in time or a focus on imagery, compared with an expansive tale taking in generations or travelling the world. Where plot is the objective, the short story has to be extraordinarily tight. One example is the work of Jorge Luis Borges (for pure enjoyment I recommend his 1970 work of short fiction *The Gospel According to Mark*). As we all know, creativity benefits from reading widely. I'll put together a list of a few of my favourite masters of the short form for the next edition, together with my reasons for recommending them.

I've enjoyed reading the short fiction submissions that have come in this summer. I have selected six very different fiction pieces for inclusion in the launch edition of the print magazine. *Betrayal* by Irish poet and writer Kate Ennals is an emotionally rich tale of family relationships. It encompasses themes of grief, alienation and unexpected connections, and beginnings and endings. The piece is written in lucid prose, and, to steal a phrase from Kate's piece, has not a word out of place. David Butler is a prize-winning fiction and poetry writer. His work of short fiction *Still Waters* is beautifully described, and vividly drawn. This is a piece in which flood water itself seems almost to become another character in the piece. Lyn Ann Byrne is comfortable in the realms of both fiction and non-fiction. Her short story *Ruby Red Never Forget* is a fluently written, atmospheric and bitter-sweet work, which focuses on ageing and the complexities of personal memory. Poetry by another Irish writer, Anne Walsh Donnelly, is already published by The Blue Nib. With *Half-a-Boy* she has produced an evocative and lyrically written work of short fiction.

Writers from further afield are also represented in this edition of the magazine. US writer Molly Fennig has written a thoughtful and well-characterized piece. I took great pleasure in reading this work of short fiction, which is wry, refreshingly different and ultimately uplifting. Finally, we include a piece of work by Sydney-based writer Audrey Molloy, best known for her poetry. Her *Peacock Blue* is taut and acutely observed.

I hope you enjoy reading all the works of short fiction selected for publication in this edition of the magazine as much as I did. Do continue to submit your works of short fiction. We will be back in December, and I will be selecting another crop of short works then.

Imogen Gladman, Fiction Editor

Announcing The Blue Nib Chapbook Contest III Winner.

The Blue Nib Chapbook Contest 3 - Summer 2018 – Results

A massive thank-you to our judge, Vivien Jones

Before we go ahead and announce the winners of the Summer 2018 Chapbook contest we would like to take this opportunity to offer our massive thanks to our guest judge Vivian Jones. Judging a contest of this calibre is no easy task and Vivien comments on this in her judge's report below. We are also taking this opportunity to invite all our subscribers to enter the next round in the series which is announced in this issue. It is important to note that all poems were read blind, so Vivien's comments are purely on the work and not on the poet.

Judge's Report:

Do all competition judges say how difficult it was the choose the winners, how high the quality of the submissions, how broad the genres, how brave the subjects tackled? Same story here. I found it extremely difficult to arrange the sixty submissions in any sort of order, or perhaps it's more accurate to say that depending which criteria I applied, I ended up with a different order each time. So I thought about the nature and function of the pamphlet as a starting point. I think of pamphlets as an introduction, often to a new voice, to me anyway. I liked that many of the submissions were semi-themed so moving from one poem to another felt like a flow. Some individual poems were captivating but didn't sit so well with the others submitted so in the end I chose the submissions I thought held together as a group.

None of the submissions were less than interesting, many of them, including several with no placing in the competition, would merit publication in any national magazine.

The 1st Placed Winner Ruth Quinlan

Judge's Comment:

I loved the simplicity of this writer's vocabulary, never narrow he/she seemed to reach for just the right word to convey meaning and emotion. In particular the fond observations of family life, in all its rawness and clumsiness, sounded honest. This collection demonstrates the value of careful recall with meticulous note of detail in everyday things - just what I would remember too, for example, in *Family Car Number One,* and otherwise in capturing moments we all experience but hardly remark, as in *Taking a Moment.*

There's lyricism in the ease with which the writer converses, as if they know their subject is the universality of joy in the everyday and there is hardly a need to indulge in elaborate language to share it.

1st of eight poems submitted

Small Acts of Anticipation

I pour boiling water into a ceramic mug,
watch tannins bloom from the paper pyramid,
restrain myself from stirring, from hurrying
the prescribed pace of brewing

I save the last chocolate caramel
from Christmas selection boxes,
freeze the last mince pies to crumble
clove-scented festivity into February

I wait until Friday to crack the seal on Shiraz,
decant to a glass, let it breathe in the humid
kitchen
before taking that first warm sip,
testing for spice and olive in a black grape

I set a timer to allow roast chicken to rest
before carving, wrapping it in tinfoil, leaving
the unopened gift dripping meat juice
onto a channelled wooden board for gravy

I bake soda bread for forty-five minutes,
then fold the loaves tenderly in fresh tea-
towels
to steam the crusts, prop them against my
granite mortar
until ready to eat, cooled, with softened, salted
butter

I see the advantages in Kavanagh's
communion
of black bread and sugarless tea, sanctity in
denial,
but I prefer the creed of postponement,
of finding small gratifications after waiting

2nd prize winner Bernadette Crawford

Judge's Comment:

These are also poems of family life, this time a family with an adopted child. The writer explores matters arising in such a family with intensity, examining the sometimes strangeness, the unrelatedness of their family dynamic, before making the child her own through the close focus of her observations, as in *I Didn't Name You,* surely the first intimacy of a 'natural' parent. In the wonderful *Queen of Snow*, the mother traces the difficult path for her black child in a largely white school until, as the star of the show, she claims her rightful place. In *I Give You Back Mother's Day*, accepting the gift of her adopted daughter she speaks to her 'natural' mother in terms of raw gratitude. These poems answer all the questions those with no experience of cultures other than their own might ask and they do it in straightforward, honest language.

1st of eight poems submitted

The Foundland

How I envied those laughing women
who came into the coffee shop
after their 'Mums-to-be' yoga class
in their bright, multi-coloured clothes.

I pictured myself in purple tights
with layers of black-and-white cotton tops
wrapped around with long scarves
and my belly swelling week after week.

All that doesn't matter now.

I didn't have a swollen belly
wrapped in colourful cloths
but I swathed you in a scarlet and yellow
chitenge
and carried you snugly on my back.

You pressed your right cheek
and your two tiny-fisted hands
between my spine and shoulder blade.
Your ear sought the love-dove

lub-dub of my heart.
I felt your heart beat too
as you tuckled down
into your woven amnion.

Together in the long afternoons
we journeyed under mango trees,
rested in the handcrafted wicker chair
to the buzz of bees busy with fallen guavas.

The current is strong
and there are many waves
to take you
to the Foundland of Mothering.

Judge's Comment:

Quite the wordsmith and has a broad reach of subject and approach.

1st of eight poems submitted

Lullabies

My arms remember.
This grandchild's soft
weight tugs.
Milky breath nuzzles,
her pearly skin part of me.
Memories of midnights flare.
I'm here and back -
a mother
in my Glasgow tenement.
On the phone-in programme
all-night souls whisper.

It's hard ... money an that ...
'specially on ma own when
the kids are down.

They're missing their Da.
He's awa - bit bother

solitary secrets
to a sleeping world.
Stars pierce the dark.

My child swaddled in my lap;
we cuddle by the bold fire.
Sparks of love flame our den,
sweet oasis in the careless city.
The DJ searches for lullabies:
high rise harmonies.

Now another bundle flashes
the same smile.
My heart: empty of secrets
my lap's cradle, full again.

Runners Up and the first of their eight submitted poems:

Amy Gordon

Field Under Stars

     The woman stands,
scythe in hand, waist-deep
in a field of grain
below her lord's castle on the hill,
     scans the sky
for the slim curve of moon
and the clusters of stars who keep
her company, along with bright Jupiter and red Mars.
She imagines they are jewels.
      Only yesterday, she believed the sun
couldn't rise without her, but this morning,
as stars go wherever it is they go,
as birds wake, and trees at the far edge of the field
turn gold, she can feel
the wobble of Earth—how it revolves
around the great circle of light.
      Her center shifts. She understands
for the first time the sun
has no need of her. She doesn't know
men will be scorned and burned at the stake
for saying so.
     She sees everything
through a new lens. Stones
of the castle are the same color as air,
and as she looks down at the veins in her hands
at folds in her apron,
her edges blur. She's no longer sure
if she's woman or wheat.

Christine Valters Paintner

St Francis and the Grasshopper

Snow falls heavy and silent,
a lake of white flakes,
Francis peers out the window,
time for night prayer,
his brothers still tucked
away in their beds.

He steps out into drifts
which reach his knees,
breathes in the icy air,
makes puffs of smoke,
arrives to the chapel
and sits and waits.

The heavy door opens
an inch, two green
antennae wave gently,
then large dark eyes appear,
long slender legs
and a soft swirl of snow.

Francis smiles at this friend
who leaps from the doorway
to land right beside him,
rubs her legs together
to create music for the psalms,
which he sings off-key.

They sit together a long time
in song and silence.

Derek Coyle

Rodin on Patrick Street

It could be a painting,
but it would probably

work best as a sculpture.
You sitting on that marble –

speckled slab on Patrick Street,
oblivious to the flow

of human traffic, babies
in prams, teenagers

skulking in shop doorways,
their headphones on;

the cars and buses, the belch
and blast of engine and horn,

while you sit back
with your Roman broccoli,

a Romanesco, its near-luminous
chartreuse,

its logarithmic spirals,
strikingly fractal,

an endless source
of curiosity to your mind.

You might feature in a Klimt painting:
your mustard–yellow

corduroy pants, green hat,
blue and gold scarf

would do the trick, but still,
knowing you, I think of Rodin

– something elegant, muscular
and grooved – although

I see you fully clothed,
sitting there for all to view.

To Lady and to Tramp

You're in love again,
and it's your first time,
it should feel natural,
as soon as lips are locked
and bra unclasped

but there's hesitation
as you wrestle with
the question of
which version of yourself you will be
the lady or the tramp.

To lady is to be reserved
in return for respect,
reliable girlfriend,
revered version of his mother

To tramp is to bare all,
reveal kinky pockmarks
of a soul that is both
ease and disease,
empty and full,
like the girls in his dreams

Dare to bare the truth
that lies inside
the deep chamber,
only emerging when
teased out in the inky black
of a curtained room
on the sanctity of a blank sheet

Or be the fair maiden
seduced by convention
acceptable to the timid
if they wish to read the story

of man making love
or love making man
or poetry

Jackie Shortland

Aspirations

You were a big part of my life
and I keep on
lighting the candles,
even if I don't believe.

In stress, I bless myself.
In distress, I say
one Our Father,
three Hail Marys
and a Glory Be,
even if I'm not convinced.

If I'm struck down
by a lorry, or a stroke,
and some good soul
thinks to minister First Aid,
with whispered aspirations
in my ear,
I know I'll be glad of it,
even if they're only winging it.

And if I'm conscious it's the end,
the devotions of a seven year old
will most likely issue out of me,
in synch with my dying breaths....

Jesus, Jesus, You have come.
Jesus, I am now your home.....
even **if** you don't exist.

M. Teresa Godfrey

Pes Anserinus
for Monica

I plan to teach myself the names of all the trees
and wildflowers of the forests and maybe even
butterflies and insects and the birds that sing
around the edges but are silent in the depths
where I go to be silent too.

This summer is the best there has been
in over forty years. I rise early
and walk 10K every day. I am alive.

In his consulting room, the surgeon splayed his hand
across his face to illustrate how my arteries, and indeed,
his and everyone else's, spread from ear to eye, and nose,
and mouth in the shape of a goose's foot and I thought
how unscientific an analogy as I realised how unfamiliar
I am with geese's feet. Though I still got his drift.

I will learn the varied shapes of leaves. I know some already –
the sycamore, the oak, the chestnut – and how to identify
all the willows that line the paths I walk.
I can see myself stopping to consult a handy pocket guide
under a heavy overhang, or bending to the face of something
so familiar I'd never thought before to ask its name.

Pes anserinus is the Latin term, he explained,
instantly giving his demo more weight before probing my face
to find its temporal branch, the one now ropey with an inflammation
that could've cost my sight. Later, in his theatre, he will snip a piece
while Johnny Cash sings in the background and I listen
to the raffia cut of the scalpel and feel nothing.

The hedges are filled with honeysuckle,
the verges rich with dog daises, buttercups, anemone.
I haven't seen such abundance since childhood.

This morning a tiny, thumb-sized wood mouse stopped in front of me.
I might have missed her among the twigs and last winter's scattered leaves
but I saw her smoothness of fur and her eyes – bright in a glint of sun –
staring up at me and I too stopped and stared.
And like this we paid our respects to the trees, the plants, the earth,
and all living things we could see and all that we will see.

Marcy Clarke

Good Old Fashioned Apple Pies

The boys, sent out early day to scold apples from knobby trees
(planted before they were born)
for Granny's pies

Morning chill
they pull the rebuilt Radio Flyer cradling an empty bushel basket
and padding, untethered, by their side
the family pit bull Hanna

Autumn sun climbs,
blushing a basket full of Honeycrisps and the dog,
sprawled in clover, one eye open doing her job
Dawdling,
they poke fingers excavating abandoned worm homes,
toss rotten apple grenades for Hanna

and crunch into fruit,
sweet juice dribbling sticky ribbons down superman sweatshirts,
wiped off on corduroy and pitty fur
Whistle from the house jostles the bully
and she worries the boys with wags and yips,
they tug the wagon, creaking beneath its dulcet cargo
to be peeled, sliced, bathed in lemon water,
wrangle a dance in cinnamon and vanilla sugar,

heaped into granny's butter crusts

and baked in her Westinghouse,
untangling bubbly scents of apple confections
teasing chilly twilight breath with farmhouse memories

Sarah Pritchard

#1 The Charity Shop Queen

Here she is again treasure hunting.
In the high street charity shops.
Drawn back into searching
for a surprise she doesn't know she wants
for grocery shopping
an excuse to reward hoard
to recycle thrift in the name of charity.

She taunts & teases herself
the books are for her isolated aunt
she's saving the planet
buying new-to-her clothes
she's donating to good causes.

It's a family disease
They all do it.
Over the years
she has had the scoop of
the back end of fashions & fads
like in the 90's it was all about fish.
Her bathroom is swimming in them.
And collections of Grannies' collections
thimbles, pigs, poodles, owls,
she imagines the Granny bought one holiday on a whim
then every family member bought her another for
all the high days of the rest of her life.
The Granny didn't have the heart to say she didn't like them.
She walks out with a tiny 60's style green & purple
ceramic donkey with huge unchipped ears.
She has always loved donkeys.
She has no children or grand children
to drown her in trinkets for
her donkey shrine.

Sheila Jacobs

I see the city through my father's eyes
Birmingham 1931

From the terraced
back-to-back
where he was born.
The poor end of town,
near Saltley gas works
and sluggish canal
under the railway bridge.

Pigeon-roost on slate
roofs, sheen of starlings
in rain-puddles, hoot
and hiss of steam trains
spiralling smoke and grit,
roar of Saturday's home
crowd at Villa Park.
Trams and buses trace
the city's inner circle,
drop workers off
at Ansell's Brewery,
Lucas's, HP Sauce, streets
humming as he meanders
to school with his mates.

They'll be fourteen, soon,
time for first suits
and steady jobs, they dream
football but know their
future's in a car factory
needing ambitious lads
eager to learn a trade.

———————

Chapbook Contest IV to be judged by Helen Mort is now open for entries. Details on The Blue Nib
site at www.thebluenib.com

New Poetry

Derek Kannemeyer

Mutt Spirituals

Ohoo, blares the blues hymn of the dog, who in his sweet gutturals of dog
howls how he's only a dog, but how he loves this language of the birds.
Baying, *Oh what it is to be a dog,*
as the alley's congregation of dogs ohoyahos amen.

Of Lucy, The Art Of Lightness, And Of Gravity

She stood in Gil's backyard, under that apple tree
Gil's parakeet once skedaddled to, & bet me she could kick her leg higher
than I or any boy could. I was 16,
she was Gil's step-cousin. New in town since the fall.
One of those first at everything blondes who tan gold in a day.
Filigreed with leaves, applauded by a bob of apples, she hiked high
her delicious thigh, that gleamed in the day's
silk light as if she'd slicked it on her skirt, & toed at the fringes of the tree;
gravely, lightly, she touched her lips to skin; she let her leg trawl
down. *Okay,* she said, *now you, come on...*
But I'd no idea what a come-on was—all pratfall
I was—all ache, & rawness—so I just kicked. I don't recall, even,
grasping that my plant foot had flown up with: only the trees'
wheel; my back smacking the grass; my shoe loosed into a sun-daze
of sky, to roost where the marauder parrot had. As Lucy high
C'ed her delight, at what she'd not known she wanted: one dumb new friend
to laugh with. I dreamed her once, shinnying in to let her gold legs loll;
toeing & dangling my sneaker in a sway of fruit. Out on her merry
limb again! My model, my fledgling years, of how to fly or fall.

Whole Day Prayer

May there be a room, this room. May there be a bed,
left warm and rumpled; a cat, this cat—caressed, fed,
cooed to, stretched dozing on his quilt. May the sunlight
under the blinds catch a little lived-in dust; not much—
let it be a neat room, mostly, in a small, neat house.
Today, we will turn the key on it, and drive—
without hurry—stopping for mid-morning coffee.
How good the scones are. And the jam, home-made!
Let the tables be small, the talk untroubled—
just the music of mill and murmur—until we close
the door on it; away. To wind, and climb, and park
where there are no cars, only this rough trail through the trees.
Until we are hiking high in the Virginia mountains.
Cloud shadow, the hover of a hawk, its contours tipped
to ride the thermals of a ridge. Or of blue-green flocks of ridges…
Let it be a month of mildness and color, April or May, say—
the way, from the valleys to the tree line, whispering into bloom;
or perhaps October, into a loveliness of decay—either would do;
are we 25 or 60?—either might do. Well, no, too late for 25—
and we lived such days at 25, let's live one now at 60.
May we take our repose upon the sprawled rocks of an overlook,
edging to peek over. And as we picnic, talk. How much
might we two have left to say? I say, let's find out.
Look, see how wide the view is, spread below us?
So where now, what next, when?
Listen, almost anywhere might do. Right here, now, for one—
perhaps even this one, warm room. We could enter it
whole-selved; we could take its whole, slow day.

Wild Quiet

You're ten or eleven, and you have this all-time favorite tree
no one knows how to find but you—
That your mother (if she did know)
would be so scared, and so scold and plead with you about
But it's away in the scraggly summer woods behind the spring
Where no one goes but the songbirds, and the night animals, and you
And the deer, and that old owl with his great skull eyes,
who barks sometimes like a dog
And when you shinny up into it, panting a little,
Scraping your skin on its knots and gnarls of trunk—
Toward where the buntings burst up out, ceding you its crown—
All the noise of you
falls—away—below
So you work and you work your way a little higher—
Past where a branch bends a bit too hard under you,
with a thrill away of leaves, and a snapped flutter—
To your next perch, and its pause, to catch your breath—
Until the shoal-shivers of the wind
enter you wholly, and they whisper,
Welcome to the wild quiet of the sky—and you are monarch of it

Appetite Song

Say me some syllables for
their sound's sake, to hear them voiced—
how playground groups shout the score
in funk-scat rhythms, fists hoist
in the air to punctuate:
Go, someone! Dibs has the floor!
Please, Mother, may I some more?

Where Form fights its border war
with Freedom, send breath to foist
on us in a blent sensate
hymn light's battle yell—to roar
the Mongrel Both incarnate.
Drive, y'all! Gas, shift, mirror, floor!
Please, feet, may I fly some more?

In food fights, the omnivore
fares best. (This squid's big & moist,
let's hurl it!) On a blind date,
savor the whole joust & joist
of things. At the hop, gyrate.
Jive, loves, till we split the floor!
Please, Sir, may june april more?

I'd rather—by all that's boist-
erous—crave *all* than *else* or
nor—garden, wide world, & gate.
Lungs, people! Roof, walls, & floor!
Please, stars, may I burn some more?

Anne Walsh Donnelly

The Confessional Box

Women cluck like hens outside the door,
they interrupt Fr. Doyle's thoughts.
Joan doesn't cluck, her voice a double bass,
her laugh, a well-tuned string.
He blinks his eyes, adjusts to the dark. The church,
this box has become his coffin.
Fingers the gold cross embroidered on the purple stole
hanging around his neck.
A John Major cough erupts from the other side of the grille,
followed by flatulence. He pulls back the curtain.
"Forgive me, Father …"
"Hello, Jim."
"Remember me telling you last week about the hard-on
I get when I go into Mullahy's pub?"
Fr. Doyle bites his cracked lips.
"It's Liz, the new barmaid, that causes it," says Jim.
The priest fiddles with the strings on his stole.
"My wife should have fixed my zip when I told her it was broken.
After Liz pulled, I couldn't get it up again."
"The zip?" asks Father Doyle.
"Yes, Father."
"So it's your Joan's fault that you fucked the barmaid."
The hens stop clucking.
Jim whispers,
 "If the Bishop heard you were swearing in the confessional box…"
Fr. Doyle stabs the wire grille.
"What would Joan do?"
Jim jumps from his knees.
"Just give me my penance and I'll leave you in peace."
"Climb Croagh Patrick in your bare feet, no walking stick."
Jim crosses his chest.
"My heart wouldn't be able for that or my gammy hip."
"Climb it twice."
Fr. Doyle opens the confessional box door, shouts at the hens,
"No more confessions today, I've an urgent house call to make."

A Tiger Called Mid-Life
After Adrian Mitchell

I have a tiger called mid-life
All she ever wants
Is to be taken on the prowl to hunt Dobermans
And spend the rest of her lifetime
Devouring their tongues

My Lioness
After Adrian Mitchell

When she was a cub,
she was happy
to play with my fingers.
I felt her twitch
at my first disco,
when I gaped at all the boys
and their little lions
tucked inside skinny jeans.
Clammy from dry ice,
she got wet when one
rubbed against her.
When I fell in love,
she opened wide, welcomed
a lion, clenched him until he filled
her with his milk.
Before long she was pushing
out babies. Lost her muscle tone.
The gynaecologist stitched her up.
Lion preferred the back door.
Wasn't as wet as she used to be.
He lost his mane.
Wasn't as hard as he used to be.
Now she plays with a lion,
powered with batteries
not lust.

Self-Love
After Mary Oliver

If you feel your heart leap
when you glimpse your face
in the kitchen window
admire the faint image that is you
feast on your beauty
dwell in your heart
don't think of self-love
as a crumb you must blow
from your table
think of it as the yeast
that will develop your dough
think of how it will nourish you
to rise
again, again
and again.

Death Is Nothing At All
After Henry Scott-Holland

Death is not –
nothing.

It is everything.

It is not –
a negligible accident.

For my mother chose
to storm
into the next room.

Our laughter forgotten.

Now, I roam derelict buildings
empty streets
screaming into the silent night.

Why couldn't God
have taken her?

Quietly.

Tom Paine

Tree Light

No one ever told me to stand in the woods and
await dusk.
But no one ever told me I'd see roots
plaintively reaching out
to me at night. No one ever told me light
flowed in limbs—
a conversation in halo sentences from tree to
tree. No one
ever told me looking at the forest floor, tree-
light bathing
bare feet, I'd weep for the trees in these dark,
dark woods

Irises

Lizzie met Gabriel. They married.
Rossetti only painted Lizzie.

No one else could paint her.
Lizzie had a stillbirth, and

died of a laudanum overdose.
The night before she died,

Gabriel painted Lizzie,
hair threaded with irises.

On the window glass, he scratched--
with Lizzie's wedding ring—

a line from his sonnet:

*"I was a child beneath her touch,
--a man, when breast to breast we clung."*

 He placed his poems in her hands,
closed the casket, drank, and died.

He dug up the sonnets first
or how could I recite tonight?

Laugh again, and go pick some irises

Cortazar

I was doing something so pedestrian
like putting things on my hotel dresser
when my phone which now works
beeped that a text came in…*from you.*
I stood by the bedside phone in hand
reading of blushing and Cortazar. I love
you for the sweetness of blushing, and:
"Come sleep with me, we won't make love.
Love will make us." I am dreaming of you,
spinning you in heels and a dress I bought
you on the left bank, or the right bank,
wherever they sell invisible silk dresses.

From a Hammock
on Grootpan Bay

It is August in the Caribbean so
there are no tourists—and Grootpan has
rocks—
sandless, it is silent even in season

it wasn't a life plan to be in a hammock
on a forgotten beach alone with
a pelican diving into blindness--

on that rainy drive down 95
you straddled hard my lap
your small nipple in my lips

a trucker's brutal air horn
signaled the end, and
I was blind for a moment

there are things we will never
have again, I remember
saying to you as we broke up

You Can't Tell Someone About Love

The streets are full of people
who have never had cancer

You can't tell someone about love.

looking out the hospital window
and the bird is the only bird

You can't tell someone about love.

people swat at love like a volleyball
sure, you've mouthed the old word

You can't tell someone about love.

love too, but now you are stricken--
the shock is not just the sickness

You can't tell someone about love.

but that the poets didn't lie and
you lived a life so cancer-free

You can't tell someone about love.

this cancer that devours your old life
until you shovel gold on your coffin

You can't tell someone about love.

and you see a wedding and think:
should I tell them about cancer?

Holiday

Down a dirt road in the woods
The river speaks in green dialects.
And two lovers clamber on a car,
strip to flesh, laughing with green secrets.
The metal roof is burning with August, still.
They drove to the woods to proclaim a green
holiday.
They are fucking as if to grow roots.
They are in a green fire. This is love.

Emma Lee

Stitching America
(for Gloria)

It started at Kansas, roughly centre,

and two strands of blue for back stitches:
the calm, smooth line of a river.

At each stitch, it felt as if she was by my side
instead of undergoing another round of
treatment.

Her remission had been short-lived.
The map spread north from Wichita to the

Canadian border
and west to Seattle and south to San Francisco,

grew major cities
and landmarks: Mount Rushmore, the Golden

Gate Bridge.
They triggered memories of holidays,

healthy times exploring new places and
textures.

Recollections increasing as the stitches did.
Lake Michigan bloomed in two shades of blue

as the map stretched
to the eastern seaboard then south to Florida,

back across Texas.
Each cross-stitch neatly railroaded. Los

Angeles the final city.
When I look at it, I see her welcoming smile.

I sent pictures of the work in progress.
Sharing urged me to finish so I could show her.

On a trip in the pine-scented valley of
Yosemite

I watched two mule deer fawns thread through
the tall grass as their mother watched the

setting sun.
I never found out what she thought of the map.

When I think of her, I see the bustle of
Cannery Row

and feel the warmth and expanse of Monterey
Bay.

When you said you'd wished you'd met me sooner

I spluttered my coffee, fortunately, back into its cup.
I don't do nostalgia. You thought I would have stopped
you making so many mistakes, I would have saved
heartache and you'd have had longer with someone who got you.

I'd have got it if you'd wanted to close the age gap
and give us a shared history of TV programmes, but
you were talking of catching me when I first moved
to Leicester. When I'd have written you off as too old.

When I'd buried myself so deep I wasn't sure who I was.
My coffee chilled. When I'd arrived with my music collection
and a file of poems, keen to move on. When I was an adult
but still a teenager and you'd reached middle management

and not yet poetry. To me, life is about making the best
of a bad job. I should have skipped coffee. You wouldn't
have loved me sooner. I pour cold coffee away.
And, yes, I wanted longer with you, but not to go back.

The Undeniable Voice
Ella Fitzgerald 25/4/17 - 15/6/96

Hers was the voice that Marilyn Monroe
lobbied
to hear at the Mocambo night club.
The voice that promoted her to bandleader
when women were supposed to be housewives.
The voice that kept her alive when homeless
after running from a step-father when her
mother died.
The voice that grew out of a church in
Yonkers.
The voice that lullabied her half-sister's child,
whom she adopted, to sleep.
The voice that persuaded Chick Webb to sign
up despite her gawky and unkempt appearance.
The voice that recorded one hundred and fifty
songs,
carried the weight of awards,
that will not be silenced by the loss of its
vessel.

L. Shapley Bassen

Unhappy Alice

Opening the hours one by one,
gifts you cannot return
though they are ugly
and do not fit.
This ingratitude
is the other side of the mirror.
Just get through the day
and looking glass.
Someone may be smiling
somewhere, somewhen, again.

Ketchup's Find

A cat named Ketchup chose their home;
his owners dubbed it Ketchup's Find.
Buoys of lobster traps bob the surface
beyond the shore this morning. July ends.
Where does the universe begin and end?
Where is its center? Wherever the cat
paces on fog feet, says the physicist,
since everything began altogether
in the beginning, banged equidistant
ev'rywhere, here near the big turtle that
is Muffin Rock, Great Wass Island,
Town of Beals, across the bridge from Jonesport,
Washington County, Maine: plot Cartesian
coordinates as August begins, while
deep beneath, pairs of ragged claws
scuttle 'cross the floor of Mistake Harbor,
and the unwitting lobsters crawl inside.

Winter

Now once again the trees are stripped
of autumn's leaves and all the other
autumns' before forgotten as well.
In winter, spring is beyond imagination
and summer beyond hope. But not only
solstice assures the return of the sun.
Bare branches uncover naked tree trunks
ugly only in contrast, beautiful in truth.
With what relief the patient feels the loss
of hair and other amputations. The past
at long last gone, the present free to becoming.
Weighing less and knowing more,
most of all the explosion of the nonessential.
We have the solar core, the white dwarf.

The Persephone False Dichotomy

http://www.nytimes.com/2013/11/12/science/space/the-view-from-saturn.html

Saturn is the god of regeneration and a timeless era of plenty and bounty before time, which he reinstates at the time of the yearly crisis of the winter solstice.

Life with Death half the year or return to Mother. Rings around Saturn
murmur warnings a four year old hears his ceiling mobile echo. How
can he fall asleep now? Mars went missing from his set. Things fall
apart, yet the center holds. In time, Malcolm will learn: his calling
by great grandfather's name; Macbeth's succeeding Prince of Scotland;
Saturn returns the Sun at cold solstice; cow jumps over the Moon.
Mother and summer go together with his father and filling buckets
with clams at the Cape. His little sister Tillie sleeps in the room next
door, and she more likely will seek and see dichotomy is false. Rings
tell the story and the missing God of War (under his bed, certainly
in the house). Would that Mars were not ever present! It's only Persephone
at certain latitudes; at poles and equator, far more elliptical.

Chocolate

Sip hot
or not.
Truffles
ruffle.
Bites
ignite.
Toppings,
I'm hoping.
The way
to say,
to show.
From sips
to lips
and know
melting.

Cathy Donelan

Those That Stir Under A Coming Moon

 A touch of gloss
lights over the wall, plants
and ice-blue sky.
Smoothed pave under
my toes, each step fills my breath
with evening cold.
Popcorn cloud, embers edge
grey dust centre rolls within,
caught between the dying sun
and curved brush of a coming moon.
Life stirs, swat of a moth
wing and repeating ticks
of a creature in the bush stills
my thought, takes the noise and
I just breathe.
A waking evening free.
Vines of ink
to lay as the bones
of a story untold.

Laying Foundations

Letters form, a phrase on the lips.
A sting of punctuation souring the words
out of my mouth,
develop
turn
bite,
swallow the syllables
back down. A vowel too empty
to paint the taste of my heart.
A consonant too tough to tell
the curls of life that come
in a restless evening sun.
Words that gnaw on the lines of my hand
deepening rivers that run through my fingers
and over my blank page.

Nora Cornell

eve:

a child as a temptress,
she lives in a garden with invisible walls
she craved what was always just out of reach,
and the saccharine fruit left her mouth sticky at the edges.
how was she to know she'd toed the line;
who was she to be a willful delinquent?
pointing fingers get caught in traps of lies,
but pretty pointed nails get farther.
she was mature for her age, said the serpent.
it felt like she was asking for it.

Names

nora is a package that fits in my palm;
the ribbon that binds it leaves no loose ends,
no confusion about my origins.
i am cornell from my mother, and
no one will guess that nora is jewish,
(says my father on the first day of high school).
nora is honor,
it is walking in with head held high,
imagining cardigan as breastplate
and topknot as helmet.
nora is light,
it is sunny-cold afternoons with friends,
running around the beach without jackets
and taking photos with golden halos.
nora is unprecedented,
the grafted branch on my family tree
which reaches high in the air but miles underground;
the rest of my name is history; it is a grounded framework
told through anecdotes and remembered in passing.
see, i am not only nora.
i am rachel for shelly, and לאה for leah,
for each pencil tip that i have snapped,
for each notebook page that i have ripped,
for each dog-eared book on my shelves,
there is a separate manifestation of myself.

The Ending & The Girl

no one thought to ask the girl –
she is young, and pretty, and the naive flower in the forest,
so she stays quiet, unquestioned and uninteresting.
or dead, depending on the ending.
no one thought to ask the girl –
if she felt scared or brave or kind,
if she felt used or empowered,
if it was dark inside the wolf,
or if his great big eyes left any light.
no one thought to ask the girl –
red-gold colorblind and dazed with sleep,
mothers were spinning and fathers had axes shaped like broken bottles,
so she wanders from church to pond to graveyard
and wonders why there are no names on the headstones.
authors have dug through every piece of dirt,
turned every stone and left no story alone.
they speculate to no one and shake their dice
until a new interpretation appears.
but in each article, in every think-piece and editorial,
in all the narratives that have begged to be built,
the girl is left alone, small and cloaked and dead,
depending on the ending.

Daily News

Today's travel ban
Includes San Marino
Just for a little variety
But, as always,
It's California
That tops the list.

Identification Invalidation

Asked: "Is she your girlfriend?" with adult smirk at imagined puppy love. Makes clear that I am a
boy and boys should like girls. But, no, I am not.

D.J. Tyrer

Hand in love

During the phase of the empty sky
when cats wore human hands
and danced on bolts of sheet lightning
in stiletto corncrakes
I spoke in hoar frost.
The fumes from the watermelon,
silly signals, turned my Adam-eating apple
to a purring citrus rapping to fangs and whiskers.
All white whole they waltzed
as fireballs and water sprouts drinking
the putrescent air and eating sweetmeats
from the milky way.

Arthur Broomfield

Re-inscribed

A year compressed into few minutes
of long and meaningful interaction,
verbal telecommunication
in a city dreading the face-to-face meetings
over chai in crowded hotels in the Fort section
of a mercantile Mumbai.
The encounters, discussions, smoking outside---now a restricted activity---
and walking down the streets on grey afternoons
whipped by a strong sea-breeze

and late evenings, accosted by fat pimps and tired street-walkers
with heavy makeup and dark rouge
the women, slim or obese,
wearing stilettos and cheap perfumes
dead eyes, swollen lips
clutching purses and hankies
wait for drunk clientele, near the stock exchange or outside
dark bars,
the mega polis now a daily canvas of greed and desire, unresolved

while Baudelaire surveys the labyrinths, inner/outer

bit foppish, talking of Poe and Monet, in the same breath,
his mind hearing strains of Wagner being played by dainty hands
of a friend

...and the honking of vehicles---loud and insistent---and the
whispering corridors
look like the innards of a dried carcass.

Sunil Sharma

Michael A. Griffith

Ash

To leave us the way she wanted, she held
her tongue, hid the diagnosis until
her illness would no longer be denied. It stripped
her power over the truth as it drank
her strength and ate her resolve.
No longer denied, the cancer became
a glutton for attention simply by being
there. Her weakness, her pains, her clenched lungs,
our tears; near-constant callers and over-staying guests.
No to therapies, no to drugs stronger than
Advil p.m., no even to in-home aides until
that last week. If the dying can't be selfish
in dying, when can they be?
No to a funeral, no to a viewing, just
spread her out around her yard
and her garden; let the wind and the rain,
the sparrows and squirrels carry her off.
If life can't take away the dead,
what is worth taking?
The last coughing, the wish for
one last smoke, sweet as
that first one, and 26 minutes later
our tears visited again.

Gem Show

Tanzanite. Dinosaurs dancing as emojis try to talk.
Charity popcorn in five flavors. Autism speaking
as several cancers spread.
Aquamarine. I care about cancer more now that we are in love,
but I still don't fear death.
Amber. Fly with me. Be still with me. Get stuck in me.
Diamond. Shine just for me. Dance only for me, Talk to me.

In Weatherly, Pennsylvania
(For Sandy Drusda)

Her trees will not last the year, she knows,
the man from licenses and safety for the city came by
and left a letter telling her to cut them down.
Tall as any she has ever seen,
these trees have seen more than five generations of weather,
winter, and warmth. Infestations and storms could not fell them
until this last bad ice, heavier than lead.
Tall but deformed now, defaced by an unkind year,
her trees try for austerity, try for the clouds, try
for strength in April's chilly winds,
as she tries to catch them with her sketchpad.
Her trees will not last much longer, she knows.

So

Picking through it all
photographs books toiletries DVDs
Scrabble letters
a weight set used twice
a wedding dress
worn once
while so young   so in   love so
scattered now thrown around torn up by
the twister of a divorce not meant to happen
to the marriage not meant to be
so
we move past we move forward we move on
we lick the wounds and learn from the scars
use them as a road map to new lives
better lives
for since we didn't kill each other we
made
each other so
much the stronger

39

Jeremy Nathan Marks

You can take my water

I have a mother a father I have a lake by my home with a dog I take to that lake I have a sister a brother and a bird that visits me each morning as we go to my lake at daybreak

   The lake is a pool in my heart my heart an island in that lake I visit my heart in water I swim its beating waters You can evaporate my water but can't extinguish my heart You might clench what is beating but you can't grasp my springs.

Time pieces

Things seen and overheard:

1992:

At a sporting event somewhere
in the D.C. metropolitan area:

"If a jury acquitted a cop of beating one of us there wouldn't be any riot."

1993:

A thirteen-year-old kid
at a religious youth event in Montgomery County, Maryland:

"They all have names like Shaniqua and Towanda.
Darnell, Sharell, and Mwaka. Names that aren't even real."

1995:

In a house in Richmond
on a youth getaway weekend:

"Oh yeah. She's got a jigaboo boyfriend. Nappy hair and bubble lips."

2005:

A few days after Katrina, at a Labor Day Weekend picnic in a backyard
of suburban Hartford:

"Did you see those jigaboos looting their own grocery stores?"

2015:

And these remarks taken from the comments section
of a YouTube video found at random:

"Hitler was right. The Blacks have nobody equal to Shakespeare."

Marissa McNamara

PA090804193714

After the tests, the cutting, your skin now a container of you and not you,
your body now a grab bag of rogue cells, we said it was good to have something

solid to say: the occlusive stop of the first c and the next syllable,
its alter personality, beginning with the softening sibilant c,

the irony of its phonetics so similar to answer. Once named, we choked
on the word that sprawled its arrogant letters across 1,000,000 papers

and computer screens and forms. Then they gave you a number
to go with the word, as if your name was not enough, as if you were a prisoner,

as if you could be scanned and sold. Soon, your consonants and vowels disappeared,
your new identity repeated until you became the narrative of a number.

Harvest

I.
They sliced sideways,
scalpel gliding horizontally
over the eye's cool surface,
curved like the earth,
and took his cornea.

II.
Where are the blue irises?
Blue the color of the shirt
I put into a brown grocery bag
with shoes and pants
and handed to the man
who showed me
casket finishes, satin linings.

III.
The mortician's magic
filled the sockets with two small cups
that propped his lids
so they wouldn't cave in,
so people could look
and tell themselves he could still see.

The Men Showed Up

with the hearts they had—
drills and saws, hammers, levels
to straighten the boards. They followed
an unwritten plan, one buried
in their DNA that told them
to set posts, hammer a floor,
raise the rails. The buzzing
and drilling and talking
outside my back door
were a steady song as they
built us a deck.

Cancer cannot erect structures.
It is too tired
from tearing itself down,
so he went out to join them:
his friends and father in law.
He sat on an upturned bucket,
watched as they sawed through wood
as if they had owned the trees.
His arms too heavy to nail
or drill, he imagined
holding the end of a board
while Mark cut, imagined
helping Michael steady a post.
And then, no longer able
to watch the deck that was to be,
he stood.

From the window,
I watched as he tried
to straighten his back,
as he paused for a breath,
as he walked slowly back
into the house. He did not lift
his sleeve to his eyes
until the door
closed behind him.

In the Belly of the Fish

A fish hangs from a chain
outside my kitchen window.
He is metal, painted blue and green.
His mouth is open as if to speak.

Outside my kitchen window the wind
bangs the fish's metal fins against the brick.
His mouth is open as if to speak.
On rainy days he sways, in winter braves the
snow.

Some days, his metal fins bang the brick—
as if he is asking to come in from the wind.
He sways in the rain, braves the winter snow
and sleet. Maybe he wants the past

and is asking to come in, out of the wind,
like he was years ago in another kitchen,
sheltered from weather. Maybe he wants the
past,
the one before my husband died and I left.

Years ago, he hung in a yellow kitchen
suspended over a table, still and quiet.
This was before my husband died, and I left
that kitchen. This morning I watch him,

now suspended over the bushes, still and quiet
with a small brown bird perched on his lip.
This morning I watch him from my window—
he and the bird, bug dangling from her beak.

The brown bird perches on his lip
then dives into his belly, down to her nest,
a bug dangling from her beak.
I stand, mug in hand, quietly watching.

She dives into his belly, down to her nest.
The fish is patient, stoic, still.
I stand, mug in hand, quietly watching,
waiting for her to re-emerge.

The fish hangs, patiently stoic and still
while she flies out again and returns.
I wait for her to re-emerge
and then, one morning, I hear their voices.

She flies in and out for days, always returns
to those tinny voices ceaselessly chirping.
I wait every morning for her re-emergence.
Their voices speak loudly to the world, almost
ready

to leave this fish that hangs from a chain,
his blue and green metal warm in the sun.
Soon they will leave their home, but for now
they grow strong in the belly of the fish.

The Math of Dying

When all the weeks
were reckoned
they totaled
the rest of his life.

Nine months a fraction
of the thirty six
predicted.

Nine months.
Enough

to grow
a person
or to produce
the number of cells
required
to kill a body.

When all the days
were added
the sum equaled
enough pain
to reach forever.

How do you measure
the length of a life?

Check off
the calendar boxes
arranged
into months, evidence
of past possibility.
Turn the pages back.
January is still there.

When the weeks
are calculated,
the total of days lived
minus the future
equals
the square area of memory.

Polly Richardson (Munnelly)

Swing

I want to drink it,
 move
clockwise around moon
I want to pack it up- take it with me
drape as if scarf
ribbon it, a bow -1st place,
nurse it as mother to new-born
and swaddle
within symphony of cow major
in the key of pigeon coo
                and lean to
                string quartet hum, their buzz
                    the foundation
                    the cement
            I want to walk into blue, brush mountain tops
                acrobat waltzing air
while prima- donna flutters silent wings
            bursting change
dotting whites softly sing
 eyes don't stop inhaling, wrestle blinks to pause
frame glitter skies slicing ebony
as she colours in dusk for tomorrow's
dream of summer rain.

Crack la la

Removing shoes in cello shadow,
fingering holes running tip to find release
inward curse till exhale, undone,
Eyes turn up, catch cloud, hold.
Remember mist on mornings sleeping was watched?
Each breath counted as colour by numbers
on my face seeped to veins,
you swim,
I walk two steps, feet always drum beat
Into shadow leaving,
Outline ribs to hip still sits- there.
I want to gorge you
Lay under conversations with constellations mapping you
No monologs
Spotlights
Other voices
Just be, licking honey.
When night calls, spoon, maybe eggs on Sunday.

Dawn Shine

Blackbird peck meticulously
I lay my skin, stretch it,
beckon the heat
Surrender my bones to the hawk eyeing,
The drought slowly rejuvenated
Blackbird peck
I dance with cloud, contorting as they do
Moving eastoverwest
        bow to all pretty hooves
to the edge of abundance blue
                J'adore J'adore
This Everest stands beneath
  tonight, curl in indigo twitch dawn- shine
 whisker dew droplet,
                    pluck fibres within

Seeds

Knife the wind, sail, come touch fingers
Build a tree a house, grace your eyes
Crimson leaves clap high.
Take a pebble, ripple waves lapping
Sow needle, bare thread- the sides of my face
Plant a seed, roots to sun – inter lock
Sapling earthed, paling green
Harvest - yellow moon,
Lay a bed, blanket translucent
Nurse to breast, sacrifice
Draw seeping curtains
Wings fan, faithfully flutter - absolution
Open window, let in stars
And bow
Bleed the cloud.

46

Kenneth Robbins

The four poems featured are from Kenneth Robbins' hitherto unpublished collection, THE BOOK OF SLAUGHTER. Each poem is drawn from a specific chapter found within the Old Testament.

Joshua 2
A Scarlet Cord

I am Rahab.
I am me.
I am no man's wife.
I am no man's daughter.
I live in my skin.
My skin lives in my house.
I rent both
to anyone who pays.
I am Rahab.
I am me.
I am the harlot of Jericho.
I am no king's whore.
I am me.

Israelites, two of them,
come from Shittim.
Two spies.
They tap on my door.
They clamber through my window.
I give them shelter.
I give them food.
I give them me.
They pay with shekels
both silver and gold.
They hide quiet on my roof
which rests within the city wall.
I keep them there.
We in Jericho melt with fear.
We know of their Lord.
He parsed the sea
as they fled from Egypt.
He dumped food from the sky
and gave them laws unlike ours.
He gave them
this land.
Our land.

They will have none other.
They will have me.

My king knows they are here.
He commands me, "Bring them out."
I do not like my king.
I do not serve my king.
I do not bend to my king.
He does not pay.
He ravages me.
For nothing.
These spies are gentle.
They are kind.
They enjoy my gifts.
They honor my skin.
They praise my house.
They pay without pause.
Save us, they say,
and we will save you.
They slip through my window.
Thank you, they say.
May we find others like you, they say.
I release them through my window.
Here, they say.
A scarlet cord is their gift.
Here, they say.
Tie this in your window
and no harm will come to you.
This you swear? I say.
This we swear, they say.
Blood be on our hands, they say,
if harm comes to your house,
if harm comes to your skin.
But if I am untrue
and tell of them,
their oath will be reversed.
This they know.
This I know.
Then be it so.
And they are gone into the hills.
They know who I am.
They will remember who I am.

I am Rahab.
I am me.
I am no king's whore.
I am me.
I do not melt in fear.
I am me.

1 Kings 17
The Miracle of Five Loaves

Elijah wasn't much of a man.
A twig with ten toes, two thumbs, and a nose.
The God of Israel lives!" he told anybody who'd listen.
"And he tells me they's a drought acoming."
Nobody paid him any attention.
"You ain't no man of God," they said to him.
"Get away from us, you Satan," they said.
They would of thrown stones at his head.
But he skedaddled best he could.

He left and on the Lord's word crept to Kerith Ravine.
He was sent there by the Lord in a dream.
Or a vision.
He didn't know the difference.
There he drunk from the brook till it went dry.
There he ate what the crows brought him till they got wise and ate it all themselves.

Bout to starve to death and dying of thirst,
he heard the Lord tell him "Get you to Zarephath where a widder woman will give you food.
"A widder woman will give you drink."
"Zarephath? Where the hell's that?"
        Exactly.
He was a man of God.
Men of God do what God commands.
Even dumb commands like going to some place that ain't on no map.

So, he wandered till he found a widder woman agathering sticks at a city gate.
"Get me something to eat," he said. "I'm starving.
"Get me something to drink," he said. "I'm adying of thirst."
"I ain't got no bread," she told him.
"Just a handful of flour in a jar and a little jug of olive oil.
"Just enough to feed me and my boy till we die."
Bout out of his mind and not knowing what to do, Elijah shrieked—
"The Lord ain't gonna let your jar get empty.
"The Lord ain't gonna let your jug run dry.
"Go, fetch me home with you and we'll fix us up something good to eat.
"I'm a man of God. You can trust me."

His thumbs made a fist.

She trusted him to hit her and hit her hard if she didn't do as he bid.
Her house was a shipping crate.
Her bed was a blanket on the ground.
Her jar was broken and her jug was a thimble.
It would take a miracle to fix even one loaf of bread from so little.
But fix it she did.
Even as her son moaned from the blanket that he called a bed.
The son was sick.
          Real sick.
Sicker than sick is supposed to get.
"You and your Lord out to mess with me," she said.
"I sin, sure, and this is my penance.
"My boy dying and my perishing from hunger and thirst."
The boy, no more than a stick with ten toes, two thumbs, and a nose, stopped his moans.
          He lay still.
          He lay cold.
          He lay dead.

Elijah blamed the Lord.
"You done this cause of me," he flummoxed.
"You done this cause I ain't good enough.
"Cause you done decided I ain't worthy."
He, same as the boy, was done in.
Finished with starving, he'd had his fill of hurt.

Even as the widder made five crust loaves from her broken jar of flour.
Even as she drew them from the stove letting loose an aroma from on high.
Elijah dumped his bony carcass on top of the boy.
He cried to the Lord, "You take him you take me, you take him you take me!"
Till he was hoarse.

He tossed on top of the boy's dead body cause it was cold.
He tossed again on the boy's still body cause it was getting colder.
He tossed every which a way cause the body was still cold and getting colder still.
          Three times he tossed.
          The fourth time the boy tossed Elijah to the floor.
Elijah shrieked. "Look, your son's alive!
"It's a miracle.
"The Lord done wrought a miracle here in this trash heap.
"Can I have his bread?

"Can I have his wine?
The widder stood amazed.
Her boy had surely been dead.
Dead and cold and deader still.

She flung herself on Elijah as he ate.
"You a man of God," she proclaimed.
"From your mouth comes the truth."
"You got that right," he said.
"You sure as hell got that right," he said.
And he ate till there was a bulge in his belly and bread crumbs in his hair.

Nobody noticed the miracle of the loaves.
They were too hungry to notice little things like that.
Besides, five loaves made from next to nothing
ain't that big a deal no matter which way you look at it.

1 Kings 1
Abishag

The King is cold.
No amount of covering
renders him warm.
Thus, I am summoned to his bed.
I am Abishag of Shunem.
Mine is an empty village far removed
from kings and kingly things.
They say I am beautiful.
I do not know what beauty is.

I lie beside him, his kingship in my hand.
I caress as my mother described.
He, the King, remains cold.
I suckle him as my mother taught.
He suckles me as she said he might.
But he remains fallow, unresponsive.
Cold

I know this meaning.
My mother taught me.
If a seed does not germinate,
it is cast aside
and new seeds are found and sown.
If a King cannot propagate
and rip through the virgin maidenhead,
then, you know and I know
what remains to be done.
With me by his side,
as alluring as I am said to be,
and he does not respond,
they say he is no longer King.
He, the King, in name only,
cannot perform.
I am insufficient, inadequate, a failure.
Since I remain intact,
am I still his and his son's to claim?

I am Abishag of Shunem.
A virgin's allure is all I might claim.
Even as that, *as that,* I am flawed.
Oh, shame on me for failing the king
Who now is king no more.

Jeremiah 1
Child's Play

I am just a kid.
Oh, heavens, I am only a kid.
I hear a voice
that I don't understand.
I complain
but no one attends.

I am just a kid.
What am I supposed to do?
The voice commands me to
share its words.
I can't, I don't know how.
I am just a kid.

Just do it, the voice cajoles.
How can I when I cannot speak?
"I knew you in the womb," it says.
Then, in spite of what I am,
the voice enters my mouth.
And I speak with thunder,
turn back the tides,
and start fires with my breath.
I call lions from their dens.
I calm torrents with whispers.
I gather throngs with my words.

The Lord of Hosts has entered my mouth.
I am armed with power.
And I abhor it.

Don't you understand?
I am still just a kid.

Nathan Fidler

Thanks To Michaela

Many thanks to you Michaela
for nurturing that seed, sick in soil,
in need of something extra.

You watched over her
so she could grow just enough
to be allowed home later.

"Der blutprobe is good."

Now she's a shady tree.
Unsteady in wind,
but capable nonetheless,

and I can stand beside her.
You were right to smile in that photo
several years later in a pool,

plucking her up once more,
checking out the little shoot of growth
beside her relieved mother.

Catch them sleeping

with their backs to the
elevated flower bed
for a nod out in the sunshine.
Getting more accustomed
with their future, where the flowers
keep them company in the minds
of their loved ones.

Scanning Obituaries

Frayed fractures in the net curtain
stood still for nearly nine months,
like Jackie's number in our phonebook.

We speculated with the empty bins
and the overgrowth in the backyard.
Shiny handrails only recently installed,
now barriers in which to spill furniture,
dark woods, popular decades ago.

Your old fridge stands guard
out on the pavement. At night
a man appears with the light from his phone
rummaging through the skip of your life.

I spy empty boxes through the hall, straining
at the back window, where suddenly
both bins are heaving with bric-a-brac.

Titan

We are the titans,
smouldering bones.

Lurid grins as we pluck
meat from the ground.

Greasy, bloody fingers,
we lick, smack and suck

until it's all gone, wiping
with the back of a hand.

功夫熊猫 2

I remember the dodgy looking cinema with
sheets
covering doorways, and card games outside.

The usher bunched the door, nodding into
darkness,
letting us shuffle through older men into seats.

Cigarette smoke hung over the screen in a
haze,
making the Chinese subtitles yet more useless.

Thankfully, Frank thought it was good,
although
he wasn't so fond of the tai chi on display.

He showed us a move on the train afterwards,
stood in the doorway, rocking between
carriages

holding and slicing a melon as we sped
our way north through the nighttime
countryside.

Roy Liran

The alleys of Montmartre

You always said we should visit Paris,
and I believed you, and one good

summer we packed two backpacks
and a dictionary, and took to the
architectural skies like post-modern

plastic pigeons. I remember how
Erik Satie walked us through the

alleys of Montmartre, unfolding
each like a newspaper, one for the
headlines, one for sports, one for

the weather, and once, on a street
corner, an accidental mime threw

imaginary fléchettes at your heart,
so I would walk the rest of my days
on the wrong side of your walls.

Seagull

The lights were bright.

Two tables carried
refreshments and hot
drinks and bottles
of juice. Everyone

arrived and found a
seat. For a heartbeat
you felt caught wingless
in the gravity of
an endless moment.

Just like a bird.

Then your words began
to preen and hop over
the lush Persian carpets.

The brick walls and the
ceiling were replaced by
a salty breeze. A tropic
sun squinted into your
unblinking eyes. Words

lost substance, swooping
to beg for handouts from
the overdressed crowd.

Like seagulls.

The ship of no return

on the stiff upper lip of a celestial
ocean, in the dim limelight of a
billion billion nuclear storms, I will
build for us the ship of no return
like a seasonal fallen leaf, floating
on currents and understated waves,
we'd gravitate in whirling calmness
towards the wells of boiling time
bare of feet we'll climb silk ladders
to dance smooth moonrock decks,
and grasp at ropes and silver chains
to dangle at the edges, and later
holding lanterns in the shade of
gossamer sails miles wide, we'll
breathe the dusty void like crickets,
bathe in liquid rhythms splashing
upwards from the keel, and drift
at last into obscurity, where nights
are long and days are new, far
from the center of the universe

Albatross

Like me, you wear
knee-low trousers
under a deeply
tanned torso. Your

salt-sprayed head
is dark brown
ruffled feathers,

just like of a bird.

In the non-darkness
we slip out of your
mother's cabin to hang
weightless in the nets
under the bow, skimming
the fluorescent waves.

We talk about the
things that come
to us. We watch an
urban chain of
glowing beads go by.

At dawn, you spread
your smiling mind
to fly ahead of me.

Like an albatross.

Charles G. Lauder

Looking Back

The moment was a colossus we built up to,
at first with wheelbarrows of sand
to mix the mortar, simple bamboo scaffolding,
then, as tension mounted, cranes to swing
sun-burnt beams into place.
When you look back at the terrace houses,
Ms Malone setting off for work,
Mr Mangera opening his shop,
it blocks the view: all you see are the builders.
Each bolt torqued floated over the city,
like a bullet out of a gun.
From my window I wondered
if today would be the day. I could not
medicate myself to sleep, I could not shit.
Would we know when the last plate
had been rivetted? Yes,
there would be silence.

Isis's Quest

She found the shoulders stretched as a
footbridge
across a stream, the eyes as ponds where lovers
swim,
the depth of the murky water hard to judge.

His fingers were the ticklish tide the clinging
seaweed
playing with her feet, his feet the thunderclap
as they pounded the earth in search of his
body.

The hair grew as wind-blown Texas grass, the
armpits
were shrubs where spiders spun webs, the
woven hairs
of his arms legs belly and back clothed the
poor,

his body's heat piped into their homes and
bedrooms.
Ears, nose and mouth were scattered caverns
where her sight and touch fumbled in darkness.

His buttocks, the curly lock above his coccyx
lived as a boar,
the pancreas and intestines as mysterious
creatures
at the bottom of the sea. The liver was a
barstool.

His heart slept homeless beneath the
motorway, his brain
served as moulded jelly at a five year old's
party, his navel
the opening of an anthill poked by anteater and
child.

His legs and arms were the colonnade of a
Greek ruin,
his neck the chopping block of a lumberjack,
his skin lay
as beach blanket umbrella, trampoline, a cup of
cold tea.

Because he had always avoided a fight his
bones,
the phalanges and metatarsals, were honed into
bullets,
his tongue was rent into a moth-eaten library
carpet

and a shag rug in a brothel. But his shape-
changing cock
was the hardest to find, button mushroom in a
field,
Big Sur sequoia, more often than not an
octopus's tentacle.

How the World is Changed

Kaplan leads the revolution, drinks straight from the keg as we congregate in old manor houses writing our manifestoes line by line. We are so poor Kaplan's jeans can't hold his balls in place. We take over the library, read Berryman and Tate, then invade the President's office who compares us to Hitler and John Wilkes Booth. We crank out a magazine, drop acid, fuck on the floor. To leapfrog ten years' experience, I pick up artists, grad students in bookstores, flings that last a week but no more. I exile myself to France after everyone else has gone and come back again.

When I return, a child's hand in each of mine, Kaplan has shrugged off the patriarchy, leads the revolution under his mother's name. They take over the armoury, the barracks, a radio station, banners and words held high. My demonstration of support is on a quieter street, very few in attendance, a couple pamphlets handed out. I am a bystander, having risen from my comfortable bed, my mayhem shushed by the crowd. Any explosion may or may not be heard by those in front. Definitely not by Kaplan and those marching past.

Kaplan is Professor, with round flimsy lenses, dark curly locks replaced with white and wiry, poised like Walter Benjamin for author photo. The manifesto, long established as status quo, showing signs of wearing thin, backwards, outdated, elitist, discriminating. A chair is named in his honor, his papers bequeathed to the library. I attend the odd gathering, share the odd idea, receive the odd glance, like a novelty wobbled off the shelf. A rare copy of the magazine is found in a second-hand shop in Toledo.

Stephen House

brutality

he's gazing into oily black
asks how much self is trapped in my now
it's disappearing
stifled can't return
i lost me to grasping lies on veiled junctions
you owe me yesterday
seeping from my real
he sneaks out need
i touch him a taste of hope
is truth fact?
hazy soul yearning mist
blind existence warming need
vibrating to quench famished reason
as we seize each other's search
i'm me under crusts you strip away to paste
back on at will
i'll ascend our lust sought mess
watch valor sprout from desperate

"stay" drones his pathetic smolder
fuelling my destitute cling
i halt my nowhere amble
grasp, hold, fuck, squirm, die, repeat
why are we screaming blind?
he leans into mute plea
stares rigid at crushed faith falling
scowls sliding shadow of youth
i was once as him

how long can we go on?
forgotten saga glides in
spun magic seeking path
of mine once all ok
alive *now stranded in crumbling wonder of*
you
next possible god
crash, shake, gasp, panic, pray, return
can't you sense noxious tears?
"fake moons shine on dearth" watching angels
sing
witnessing recurring snatch at waning loss

we crawl
hushed moans sealing secret sinking dread
feigned respite tickles burden
rising dawn spurts clutched belief
he kisses my beg
holds desire in mortal ransom
don't smash my gift of me
fright feeds incapable escape
he passes wine
skull, reach, vomit, drop, writhe, relapse
shared anticipation compulsion
disintegrating to re-emerge
how long have we been drinking?
he flicks me anonymous pill
"swallow it baby"
ingest his present lie
thrust tepid flesh at me
drive hard inside me
beard scrape sunken face
drown threadbare identity
bury emerging demise
gulp, breathe, swallow, lick, plunge, reload
explode manufactured parody
spinning
trapped in web of helpless
he's peering into icy grey
asks how much life is saved in my here
it's gone
slaughtered won't revive
still you reel me back from flee
hurl disguised span of hallowed lure
i clench on
floundering
in attempting remains
as smidgeons of enduring wish glow
entombed
in your brutality

Daddy

I find courage and go to the road of my Daddy;
breathe deep crossing industrial wastelands
as smoky grit envelopes me, as trucks spew
dust in my mouth and eyes,
and angry men on motorbikes hurl toxic glares
in my anxious path. I pass scraggy scum
gathered
in mouths of dark tunnels gesturing me back to
play the game;
ignore lurking, leering ghouls who croak at me
in ghastly need.
I flee from all I was before but now leave far
behind.
Daddy is sitting on a wooden crate outside
of a shut-down factory on his garbage-strewn
street;
his footpath bed beside him; smoking joint,
sipping
on warm can of beer; engrossed in watching
a scrawny dog picking through an overflowing
bin.
I sit next to him. "Daddy, I came to see you."
He offers me a puff of weed. I shake my head,
no.
"Daddy, I need to ask you why? You have to
tell me;
give me that if nothing else. Why you never
tried to find me?
Why it was left to me to seek you out, to see
if there was any part of you in me; to discover
that absent piece of cruel jigsaw I could never
complete;
to know if you were more than her and the shit
she dished out daily? Daddy, I want to know
why
you didn't find me to give me what I craved?"
He stands and paces; stops and bangs his filthy
hand
on loose, graffiti covered tin. "Daddy, stop that
fucking noise!

I want to know why?" He doesn't answer; ends
his racket
and slumps back down.
We watch the dog rip apart a dead chicken it's
dragged
from the bin; glazed eyes and greedy mouth
gulping
feathered flesh; slimy blood spilling
over speckled, poultry pattern; "Tell me," I
beg,
and rest my hand on his bony, tattooed arm. He
looks into me.
I sense his sadness so real I see him for the
first time.
"Daddy, is that you?"
"I don't know why I didn't find you," he
mutters in disgrace
and shuts his eyes tight.
The dog skulks away; chook remains dribbling
from crimson mouth. We sit still; hand in
hand; my Daddy
and me. He's crying. I kiss him on the cheek,
stand
and walk away. And with strength I have never
felt before,
I say goodbye to my Daddy... forever.

Baik Manusia

in my street they call me *Pelacur*
Prostitute
i've heard them whispering
woman who sells fruit asks me if local men pay well
she sees guys visit my room
i could explain we hook up just for fun
no exchange of cash
but i smile and say nothing
local men love sex with *Bule*
Foreigners
and foreign men are into them
we're at it all the time here
coupling up in all kinds of crazy ways
fucking and sucking and kissing and hugging
blowing alien loads as gifts for each other
i wonder if the rest of the world know
how much men from different cultures fuck
secret inter-race fucking all over the place
bringing peace to the planet
in a pleasurable way
people in this street know
they call me and the guys who visit *Homoseks*
Gays
i've heard them muttering
they also smile
and call me *Baik Manusia*
Nice Man
i've heard them murmuring

thank-you watchful neighbours
Homosek Baik Manusia
Gay Nice Man
it could be worse than that
but one word is not completely correct
Pelacur
Prostitute
i'm not that
anymore
unless i'm desperate for *Uang*
Money

dead men's clothes

dead men's clothes hang sadly limp
in a world of once-worn wares
beaten by time in her tin shed shell
she rubs her eyes
blinks twice
gapes
smeared pink lipstick
pasty rutted face
cloudy eyes of stance in age
acceptance of a sort
into her desert store of what remains
i have come on my meandering way
threadbare fear of disintegrating middle age
another tick in time
lonely icy day
muddled from substance
coming down
no room or bed tonight for me
or friend or family near
i try a humble vest of era long gone
add a coat of wool in olive grandpa green
she smiles slightly knowing hint
at where i may have roamed to be

fingers sleeve with bony stroke
no one comes here anymore she says with stare
once it was different she breathes silently
desert queen won't see me pay
gives sincerely her woven generosity
holds lost dreams in wrinkled brow
set in stone her quiet tenacity
our chalky selves meet and we freeze within
our haze
knowing well our mortality
reality of humanity
i am warm now walking my never knowing
way
another vacant dustbowl extremity
i slow to stop
glance back
safe in mothball tweed
she waves from pebbled path
outside of her reality
and in my dead men's clothes
i signal back a simple nod
another moment wise
victorious
wandering alive

café of then

there's a café tucked in a city nook
where i'd regularly be decades ago
when i'm back this way i always drop in
take my once table spot
float back to life of then
i'd skulk here to hook up late at night
drop in heading home in wide eyed dawn
speeding crazy
crashing low
nowhere to go
needing somewhere be
boy dream soaring
hard morning pain
confused by not real
escape bad trick danger
a mate from that epoch arrives
i nip in and order bitter blacks
bump into a bloke with now grey hair
who i knew from more than here
shakes hard my hand
recalls with worn grin
us in a dim city room with new-found trade
working together a few times one year
i chuckle wry at on the game ways
he sniggers sly at what's not forgot
and as years slide on
and ways of vanished youth drift into psychedelic space
i give thanks to run-away eons of after dark lads
who faded out through fate and choice
or kept roaming on like me and some
grasping spontaneous memories
jolted along in almost old age
holding blatant facts of dwindling time
hidden stories of bygone reality
steering the remembered route
back to this café of then

in savage dark

for eight vulnerable months
i rode the well-worn wagon
of almost straight and clean
but i leapt off
with zest in need
morphed into my magical maze
i revel in time revile
messy substance games
i don't know why i play
please don't snag me back and back
i beg to somehow stronger
that must hear and comprehend
when i stand proud in real
on the wobbly sober carriage
of hope entwined with fear
i am that man i really am
innocent of my psychedelic diversion
i smile genuinely
not babble on in flooded dreams
dancing days away with invisible trickery

of my muddled mind in soaring guess
with soul damp numb in body brittle
so i crawl back on the not so trusty wagon
feeble from swimming in the swirl
and trembling i stretch up
towards new beyonds
above sneaky hypnotizing temptation
quietly caressing crumbling me
crying hidden tears of disintegrating optimism
but attempting clarity
with all that pleads within
i will be ok believed as pray
in my sickening familiar way
stunned awake in savage dark
reduced to nearly zilch
by my internal affliction
but slowly healing
nearly living
in real of now

New Fiction

Betrayal - Fiction by Kate Ennals

"The doctors say he has weeks left, if that. One of us has to go."

I was with my older brother, Sam, in a café in St James' Park, London. My father was dying of cancer in Canada, somewhere in the vast, great plains that dominate the mid-west territory.

"Will you go?" I asked Sam.

"You should. You are closer. Beth is going on Friday. She can help you with Cian."

I sighed. Beth was my father's mistress, or lover, as she preferred to be called. Last year, mum had left dad after 37 years of marriage. Apparently, Beth had been the last straw in a long line of women. Everything appeared amicable. Not a word out of place. They sold the family home and bought two separate apartments. We all met for dinner every so often, usually in restaurants. No-one passed any remarks. Then Dad got diagnosed with cancer and, after initial treatment, took up a visiting professorship of Human Rights in Saskatchewan.

"We can get your plane tickets tomorrow," Sam said.

"Can't you go? It's so difficult for me with work and the children," I pleaded.

"I can, but you would regret it."

I nodded.

Three days later, Beth, Cian and I boarded the aeroplane. I hadn't been on a plane for years. I watched London dissolve into lego-land. Beth ordered gin and tonics. A thrill of pleasure trilled. It was a relief to get away from the pressures of work, children, marriage. Then I felt guilty. I must focus. I was going to watch my father die.

Five hours later, as the plane descended into the red painted leaves of Montreal, Cian screamed. His face screwed up, beef tomato like and his tiny fists lashed out. I watched his temple pulsate.

"Do you think he has burst his eardrums? Planes can affect babies' ear drums."

"I'm sure he is fine," said Beth, with little interest.

"Please stop," I whispered to Cian, desperately rocking him. Finally, we landed. Cian's sobs subsided into gulps of air, like mine.

"We're late. We have to run to make the connection," said Beth. "Come on."

In the baggage hall, Beth's suitcases arrived straightaway. We waited for mine, Beth tapping her foot.

"We're going to miss the connecting flight," she muttered.

Cian started to whimper. He must be hungry. I was wondering whether I could feed him while standing when I saw my bag.

"That's mine!"

Beth grabbed it.

"Come on."

"I have to wait for the buggy."

I watched Beth's impatience play out on her face. Her cheeks flushed to the roots of her red hair, her grey eyes flashed and her nostrils flared. I turned my back and watched the carrousel. Only a square brown cardboard box with white postal stickers circulated. Cian started to cry. I was going to have to feed him.

"I'm going on."

I turned around in surprise and before I had time to say anything, Beth strode off. I watched her auburn curls bouncing up and down as she disappeared. I couldn't believe it. I hugged Cian close.

"Wow!" I said. "Cian, what do you think?"

I looked down at him. As usual, when calamity struck, Cian had gone to sleep. Finally, the buggy arrived. I laid Cian gently on the ground while I put it up. I strapped him in and balanced the bag on the top. B32 was the departure gate for the Saskatoon plane. I was in terminal A. I hurried off, pushing the buggy with one hand and carrying the suitcase in the other. I tried running but it was difficult to navigate the crowds. It was hot and heavy. The large square, black and white floor tiles slipping beneath my feet made me feel dizzy. After five minutes, I got a side stitch and had to slow down. A prickly heat grew in my cheeks. Maybe if I put the suitcase in the buggy and carried Cian, it would be easier. I stopped and swapped Cian for the suitcase. He was lighter. I looked at my watch. The Saskatoon plane had left five minutes ago. I stood still, surrounded by strangers going in all different directions. Dad was dying and I felt like I was drowning in an airport. What now? I took a breath. Oh God. Grow up, I thought. You're an adult. You just get another ticket. You have a credit card.

"Ok, Cian," I whispered. "There's always another 'plane, isn't there? Let's go to the gate and see."

At least I no longer had to run. How could Beth have left me? Dad wouldn't like it when she arrived without me, I gloated, but I didn't like the thought of her standing by his bed, when I arrived, already in situ, smiling. And suppose I didn't get there before he died. Suppose I couldn't get a flight. Stop it, I told myself. One step at a time.

As I approached the gate, it was busy, people were milling around. Surely this wasn't for the next plane, already. I scanned the crowd for a glimpse of Beth's auburn curls. When I saw her, I couldn't help feeling a rising tide of satisfaction while at the same time wanting to cry with relief.

"The 'plane is delayed," she said sheepishly. "Sorry."

"Thank God."

I hid my consternation, busying myself with the baby change bag and mat. Cian was soaked and my sleeve was wet from carrying him.

"I am sorry, Kath. I lost my head. I shouldn't have left you."

I nodded, changed and fed Cian, cooing and caressing him, while tears poured down my cheeks. I couldn't control them.

Five hours later, we arrived in Saskatoon. It was mid-evening but still bright. We caught a taxi to Dad's rented flat which was in the basement of a concrete corner apartment block. The sitting room had a nylon, paisley-patterned, carpet of red and orange and the wall paper was brown and mottled. The windows were high up and pavement level with the street. In a letter, Dad had described his accommodation as giving him a 'worm's eye view of the world.'

"Oh, my God! Dad tarted up the flat a bit in his description. Look at the mock orange and green fur on couch."

"The plastic furniture is awful," said Beth going straight into the kitchen.

"It's miserable. How could he have lived here?" She called to me.

"He said he could get nothing better."

"Are you joking? Did you not see the gorgeous houses down the road?"

"I don't think he had enough money. The separation from mum probably caused a dent in his finances. He doesn't have an income yet from the University. Presumably it doesn't pay him until October when term starts."

I felt irritated that Beth didn't know about his money problems. I rubbed noses with Cian on the floor while changing him and tickled him but then, I hadn't realised how broke Dad was either. I shied back as I got an electric shock from the baby.

"Cian is full of electricity from this nylon carpet!"

Dad's room in the hospital was small but light. It overlooked the tall, red brick chimney of the morgue. He looked like a living skeleton. I gave him a kiss on each flaccid and florid cheek. Chaucer's Miller's Tale came to mind; his 'neck slacketh'. My big father had shrivelled. Bones protruded.

"How are you, Dad?"

"All the better for seeing you, and Cian. Let me look at him," he said in a jovial voice. I held out my son to him. Dad looked rather than taking him.

"Now, there is good health for you! He is beautiful. Very bonny."

He held out his hand to Beth.

"Hello, love. A good trip?"

I let Beth deal with details of the journey. She mentioned nothing about abandoning me.

"Great view, Dad, the chimney."

"I know, I watch the sinners go up in smoke."

"Oh Dad. We'll have to get you out of here."

The next day the nurses suggested we take him out for the morning. They attached oxygen canisters and drips to the wheelchair and wrapped him up. It seemed wrong to have my dad wrapped in blankets in a wheelchair. It was a beautiful, clear, autumnal day. The sunshine was high in a blue sky and there was a sharp, fresh bite in the air. Beth wheeled him while I pushed Cian in the buggy. I felt as if I had ventured into Alice in Wonderland.

"Got one of them for me?" said Dad pointing to Cian's hat and scarf. I hadn't thought of him needing scarves.

"Of course," Beth answered. She wrapped him up in her black scarf and woolly hat. I thought of him scrabbling over the Welsh hillsides in sandals, rolled up sleeves, arms grazed and bleeding from the 'short cut' through the brambles.

"Lovely day!" I said.

"Oh, what a wonderful morning…" Dad began to sing.

"Oh, what a beautiful day…" I continued.

"Dad, what about that song, 'It's the same the whole world over, it's the rich wot get the gravy and the poor wot get the blame.' Let's sing that."

We continued through the roll call of songs that we used to sing in the car on family holidays. Beth knew them all too, though she had a few different words and harmonies in places. We laughed at the occasional flat note. It began to feel like being on holiday.

"How does that song go…'Red Fly the Banners O'. You know, I'll need you to write down the words of these songs, Dad… " The implication sliced through the sharp, cold air. "…I didn't mean it like that." I couldn't think what to say to make it better.

"I've already started, love. You'll find them in the desk drawer."

He started to cough. I put my hands over Cian's ears. I didn't want him to hear. We returned him to hospital and we went to the worm's lair.

70

The days and nights spilled into a routine. Every morning I would take a few minutes in the bed I shared with Cian, playing. Then I would shower, having to swill handfuls of my long hair down the plug hole afterwards. I fed Cian a jar, wrapped him up and put him in the buggy to walk to the hospital looking at the beautiful turreted houses. I would spend the day with Dad. He slept. I read or cuddled Cian. Every day I spoke to the social workers, and hospital authorities. I wanted to fly dad home. But because he was dying, no airline would take him. Beth would come in about five and stay with him overnight.

At six in the evening, I would walk home again. I couldn't get over how everything was so regimented. You had to park your car on the right-hand side of the road, facing the direction of the traffic. You were not allowed to cross the road except at pedestrian lights. You were not allowed to eat or drink on the street. Some blocks were for apartments, other blocks were reserved for houses. There was no mixed tenure. There was never a wrapper or piece of rubbish knocking about on the wind.

There was a group of doctors on the hospital ward: the Cancer Doctor, the Blood Doctor. The Heart Doctor. The Lung Doctor. One day, together, en masse, they approached me to consult. They told me that he was going to die very soon. Despite knowing this, after all, it was why I was here - to be with him when he died – I was shocked. I watched myself from a distance, talking to the doctors. The real me was hovering to the left, about three feet off the ground, like Lewis Carroll's Cheshire cat. I examined their faces, noting the brown eyes of the Cancer Doctor and his red sideburns. I wondered what his home looked like. Was it an apartment or one of the lovely big houses? Probably an apartment. I looked for a wedding ring. His fingers were bare. I could hear what the doctors were saying but I couldn't focus. I wondered if they were well paid and if, when dad died, I would have to organise a dead body on the plane. Did the doctor have a family that he would tell about his day? About my dad dying, about me, about my response. I suddenly realised I'd better make one. They were waiting.

"Thank you. You have all been very kind."

I went back into Dad's hospital room. Like a child, I felt puffed up with my important news. I stood at the end of the bed, holding the iron bedstead. I needed the cold metal to grip. At least, I thought, I didn't suck my fingers any more. The iron taste in my mouth used to be horrible after fingering metal. Tears begin to sting the back of my eyes. I took a deep breath. Deep, deep, breath. I must be strong. I breathed out slowly. Another deep breath. Then I spoke but I heard my voice quaver. I blurted it out, like a teenager.

"The doctors say that is unlikely that you have more than a few days to live, Dad."

I moved to the side of the bed and took his hand. I tucked my fingers into his, in the special way that we had since I was a little girl and he woke me at dawn to take me to Hampstead Heath on early morning walks. He opened his eyes. They were still blue, but watery and pale. The skin hung on his cheekbones. His eyebrows, though, were still bushy at the ends. They were flying off in all directions. He squeezed my fingers.

"What a cock up!" he muttered.

"They say he's only got a couple of days left," I whispered to Beth in the corridor when she arrived.

"Have you told him?"

"Yes."

"What did he say?"

"It's a cock up.

71

"Has he said anything else?"

"No."

"It's so frustrating," moaned Beth. "I thought it would be different. I wanted to be with him. But I'm not. I'm with a stranger!"

"Oh Beth!" Horribly, I was pleased to hear this. It meant she was not as important as me. Then, I felt guilty. How ridiculous to have these competitive feelings.

"I'm glad you are here, Beth. I don't know what I'd do without you."

And I meant it. I gave her a big hug.

"Let's have time out and go to the liquor store on the way back to the flat tonight and treat ourselves" I suggested, "I think we deserve a drink."

Beth smiled.

"Good idea! Let's eat together. I'll cook."

Bizarre, I thought, now we were celebrating!

We left the hospital early and returned to Dad's lair together. Beth cooked in the kitchen while I prepared Cian's supper, changed and bathed him, and finally put him to bed. I went back into the kitchen, waving a bottle of wine and two glasses. It was a relief to have a break from the usual grim routine.

"Something smells wonderful."

"Nearly done," said Beth. "Give me ten minutes while I wash."

Over supper, we discussed Dad. Silly stories and memories flowed with the wine and by the second bottle, we were sharing secrets. The nylon carpet provided a soft glow and warmth. The fake fur began to feel soft and cuddly. We made each other laugh.

"You know when he joined us skiing last year, he refused to wear the proper gear. He insisted on wearing his old corduroy trousers and old wax jacket that he always has. He looked ridiculous and it was awful when he fell into ten foot of snow. We had real difficulty getting him out."

"People loved your father. He would walk into a room, and everyone would try to gather round him."

"He was quite scary though, when I was child. His eyes would pierce blue, his mouth would shrivel and his voice would freeze. He smacked me once when I swore."

"He didn't want to leave your mother. But when she left him, the vultures descended…

"He told me. And you won. Well, I'm glad."

We laughed, drank and smoked away the night. Occasionally, I thought of mum. How she was at her flat at this minute, sitting alone, waiting to hear from me. I felt a stab of guilt about sharing his death with Beth. I was enjoying this. It made me feel close to him. It kept him alive. I was glad it was Beth with me rather than mum. It was mum's fault for refusing to fly out. If I was friends with Beth, they were to blame. They should never have split up.

At the hospital the next morning, after I had settled Cian for his mid-morning sleep, I sat with Dad.

"I want all the medicines and drips stopped," he said shortly.

There was silence while the words found a resting place in my head. At first, I was shocked, then relieved. When I realised my relief, I felt guilty and then worried that my face was betraying these different emotions.

"There isn't any point in lying around," he said, "might as well be done with it."

"I'll talk to the doctors."

I walked quickly out of the room.

72

In the corridor, I could hear the doctors doing their round. I watched them coming towards me. Their footsteps clicked on the floor tiles as they approached. Click, click, click. I clutched my hands behind my back. I dug my nails into my fingers. Pleasantries were exchanged briefly. Then, slowly and deliberately, I spoke.

"Dad wants to turn everything off. He doesn't want to wait."

I could feel the tears welling up. I squeezed my nails harder into my fingers. Half of me felt like an unhinged adolescent and the other half trapped in the straitjacket of an adult. There was no hovering outside my body this time.

"We need your permission. And his."

"You have mine. Is it possible? How long will he last without medication?"

Talking practicalities helped me steady my voice.

"It's difficult to say. Maybe a day. We can keep the morphine going," said Dr White, the cancer doctor. "I will speak to him."

We entered his room. The chimney stood tall in the window. Not smoking today. It would be, I thought. Dad opened his pale blue eyes and gave a small smile. One I associated with him when he was angry.

"Hello, doctor. I would like everything turned off".

While weak, his voice still contained a frisson of the sternness that used to make me quake. The doctor nodded.

"We can keep the morphine going," he answered.

Dad nodded.

"I will arrange it."

"Thank you."

I watched the exchange. My head turning from one to the other. Wimbledon popped into my mind. Dad and I loved Wimbledon.

It was that simple. Dr White looked at me and we left the room. My nails were still digging into my fingers behind my back. The tears flowed down my cheeks anyway, regardless of my embarrassment. I tried biting my lip.

"They will stop the medication this afternoon," he said. I nodded, unable to speak. He walked away. I heard his heels click. Then I watched him turn and come back to me. He took my hands from behind my back. My palms were bleeding.

"I will leave a prescription for you."

I nodded.

After a while, I phoned Sam.

"I guess it's time you and Dad started making phone calls," he said.

Phone calls? Sam said Dad would need to phone people to say goodbye. I realised this would include my mother. Was this necessary? I wondered if Sam was asserting his authority from afar. I returned to Dad.

"Sam says we have to make some phone calls, Dad."

We both looked at the phone which sat on the side of the hospital bed. I dialled mum's telephone number first. It rang for a long time. Finally, she answered. Her voice was high pitched, trying to be calm. I couldn't bear to talk to her.

"We are both here. I'm fine. I'll put you on to Dad."

I made to leave the room. Dad beckoned me back.

"I'm fine, love," he said into the phone. "Everything is fine. It's a bit uncomfortable. No, there is nothing I need. Are you all right? Good. I'm a bit breathless. Look after the grandchildren. Take care, love."

Was that it? I wondered. After forty years of marriage. No one else was in. Thank God. I left messages on answer phones. "Hi, just Kath here. I'm with Dad. We wanted to say goodbye."

The next morning, I arrived early. He was still conscious.

"Good morning, love."

He closed his eyes and squeezed my hand. I tried to think of encouraging things to say but I didn't think wittering on about my early morning childhood walks with him and Rusty, our dog seemed appropriate. He probably had more important things to think about. He slept, I think, or maybe he was unconscious. Beth arrived at 4pm. We sat, one on either side of the bed in silence. I left with Cian at 9pm and went home to bed, exhausted. At four, Beth rang.

"He's dead."

"Oh God! Did he say anything?"

"No. There was a rattle and he shook a bit."

I hurried to the hospital. It was just getting light. A white light. The streets and the usually busy hospital were deserted. Silence. I walked in. Everything seemed so deliberate, defined. I noticed scratches on the floor. I had a strange feeling of drama. I hurried to the room. Beth stood by the window. Dad's body looked waxen.

"They've tarted him up.".

"What did they do?"

"Straightened him out, and put some kind of make up on him."

I looked at him closely and touched him. He had gone.

"Let's pack his stuff and get out of here."

My voice broke. I felt wretched. I'd never see him again. I was furious.

Back in the lair with a worm's eye view, Beth opened a bottle. We toasted Dad. Raising my glass, I said.

"To dad's cock up."

"I'll drink to that," Beth laughed. I grimaced. I hadn't meant it like that.

We left the next day, me holding Cian and carrying Dad's hot ashes under my arm. I left the remains of his stuff to the worms. We flew to Alberta and from there to Heathrow. I left Beth at the airport, and never saw her again.

"It was horrible, mum." I said, though I knew that wasn't wholly true. "I'm glad you weren't there." Sadly, that was the truth.

Still Water - Fiction by David Butler

After the estate flooded for the third time, Clodagh determined never to return. The thought of the dank interior, silted and filthy, filled her with reptilian loathing. She left Becky in care of her sister; was seen moving like a sleepwalker along Bridge Street. Before striking out in the direction of the weir, she placed the front-door key in an envelope with only the address scribbled on it and pushed it through the bank's quick-deposit shoot.

The speed of the first flood had been chilling. In the space of a night hour, the water had swollen from runnels leap-frogging the tarmac to a waist-deep inundation upon which boxes, toys and furniture bobbed and bumped. In the pale halo of a hand-torch, a fridge (was it?) rolled its flippant back. So sudden had the upsurge been, so overwhelming, that neighbours half-dressed waded in and out of unlit houses, laughing, scarcely knowing what to save and what to abandon. She'd shivered on the high ground in pyjamas and dressing-gown, soothing the baby, watching the efforts of Kyle and the others with a detachment that was, almost, amused.

For weeks not a single resident of the estate had been able to return. Long after the waters receded, walls stripped of tide-marked wallpaper exhaled a river-breath whose alluvial taint blow-heaters failed to dry entirely. Once the insurance assessors had ticked their peremptory clipboards, carpet and underlay, lino and flooring had been pulled up and dumped over the limbs of chairs and prostrate tables in great communal mounds to the head of every terrace. Only the electricals had been taken away for specialist disposal.

At least it had been a shared catastrophe. In the hostels where those without options were variously lodged, a grim camaraderie prevailed. Besides, the inundation had been countrywide; an event which the forecasters declared a once-in-a-century occurrence. If compensation was slow in coming and not remotely commensurate with actual costs, the cheques went some way toward restoring morale. Neighbours began to talk up that night as a disaster-movie they'd all survived, a shipwreck in a midlands town. There was much talk of a communal lawsuit which, as months went by, failed to materialise. Late November, on the anniversary, Clodagh's terrace held a party out on the common that was enlivened by fireworks.

In spite of the freak weather-event the forecasters had described, the new premiums had either shot up exorbitantly or else contained a clause that excluded compensation in the case of flooding. This was the occasion of the first real dispute between Clodagh and Kyle. For an American, Kyle was cautious. Arguably, it was his careful temperament that had landed them on the new estate in the first place. She'd wanted the semi-dee out on the Dublin Rd that would, admittedly, have stretched their monthly repayments above the fifteen hundred they'd fixed upon. That said, the sixty thousand down was her money, a legacy from her mother. The property would be in her name. She should have gone with her instinct. But Kyle could do no wrong in those days. Besides, she'd been pregnant, and who knew what unexpected costs a baby might entail.

His caution notwithstanding, it was she who now argued for the extra cover. Kyle, with trademark smirk, attempted to play down the mathematical chances of another inundation with an argument an infant could see through. She knew damn well you couldn't 'times it by a hundred, Clo, just do the math. We could buy a couple more houses for that kinda dough.' At the same time, a fivefold hike in the premium payment was outrageous. It would be difficult to meet, particularly now her maternity leave was unpaid. Rebecca was a strange, interior child – later, she'd be diagnosed as 'on the spectrum' – and needed a care Clodagh was loath to entrust to strangers.

Her stubbornness on the point surprised Kyle. She'd always deferred when it came to matters financial. 'Honey, I know you're upset, but come on…'

'Tell you what we'll do,' she said, brightly. 'We'll ask Dee.'

'Dee? What the hell's Dee got to do with any of this?'

At least Dee works up in the Financial Centre, she thought. She didn't say it. Nor did she bring up the semi-dee on the Dublin Rd. She waited until he'd set off for work, then Skyped her sister.

After the call she felt deflated, even humiliated. Deirdre agreed with a roll of her eyes that of course you couldn't 'times it by a hundred, just do the math.' She'd never thought quite so highly of Kyle Bradley. That said, what it came down to was Becky. To meet the sort of excess Clodagh was talking about, she'd have to go back to teaching fulltime. Bar everything else, that fivefold hike (fivefold? Jesus!) was out of their reach any time soon, with so much refurbishment still to be broached. Face it, darling, he's got a point…

'Ok,' she said to Becky, once the computer screen went black. 'But I can't say I'm happy about it.'

Four years went by before the second weather-event. In the interim, Clodagh discovered a talent for economising. It became a fixation. It was born of necessity; the school where she'd taught, though most understanding, could no longer hold the position open for her. When Kyle was away, she thought nothing of illegally strapping Becky into the baby-seat beside her, collapsing the rear seats and driving ten or even twenty miles to a house-clearance or a car-boot sale. She became adept at surfing the second-hand websites and second-guessing which were scams. She ended up sourcing bargains for half the terrace.

She began to smoke, something she hadn't done since college days. She put together a glasshouse and tool-shed. And in face of Kyle's hoisted eyebrow, she developed a real knack for D.I.Y., and even earned the respect of the floor-hands in Woodie's. With business taking Kyle increasingly back to the States, she had something of a free-hand about the house.

There was no lack of warning this time round. If the first flood had stolen in like a thief in the night, the second arrived with the inevitability of an advancing army. All summer – it was the wettest on record – a swollen sky had loured over the entire country, dumping its excess onto an earth already saturated. For days as she'd walk Becky through the fine drizzle along the river, Clodagh had watched with tightening gut the bloat current squirm between the banks like a restive anaconda. Toward the town, teams of men in hard-hats, the Fire Brigade, and even a truckload of bawdy soldiers had begun to bolster the flood defences with sack upon sack of wet sand while a pair of yellow diggers like monstrous toys rattled to dredge the riverbed. High time, because with each bulletin, the contour-maps tracked the gradual approach of a double-depression across the Atlantic.

On the Thursday she called Kyle. He was in Portland, Oregon, in all likelihood unaware of the impending disaster. As it happened, he wasn't unaware. He'd been keeping abreast of developments on the net. 'Honey you know what time it is?'

'Yeah. Listen I need you back here.'

'Huh?'

'It's happening again Kyle. It's going to happen again.' Silence. Static. 'I can't cope alone.'

'What about Dee? Hun, move in with Deirdre till the worst is over. Will you do that for me?'

'Kyle. We need you back here.'

A long silence. 'No can do.' She waited. 'I told you this, baby, I explained I…' But what it was he'd told her he didn't get to repeat, or if he did, it was into a deaf cell-phone.

She spent Friday emptying cupboards and presses, hauling what could be moved up the stairs to Becky's room, or her own, or the bathroom. She hauled boxes filled with linen and books, CDs and pictures. She hauled up lamps, the TV and the music-system. She rescued the dinner-set, the espresso-machine, the kettle and microwave. The fridge she emptied into a Tupperware drawer which she laid in the bath alongside the perishables and foodstuffs. A number of times, she sat inert for so long that Becky tugged at her. It wasn't from exhaustion, precisely. Her eye would fix unseeing on the washing-machine or the cooker, on the glasshouse or tool-shed, on the sofa or the fireplace or the parquet floor, her mind vacant. Dee, who'd driven all the way from Dublin straight from work, collected Becky and a bag of her things; Clodagh scarcely roused herself to thank her.

That evening, and through the night, the terrace mounted its own vigilante action. Civil Defence had deposited several van-loads of sandbags and booms which they worked to plug up each gate and doorway to the height of a child. On their macs and umbrellas, the persistence of rain was pure sound. Only within the wasp's nest about each streetlight were the orange darts momentarily galvanised. It was hard to comprehend how they presaged a deluge.

There was markedly less humour this time round. Laughter was nervous and mirthless; cordiality strained by those pulling less than their weight, those occupied with their own properties to the exclusion of all else. The river was due to peak in the early afternoon. If the riverbanks could contain it, or if the overspill was limited, the glutted beast might just pass the estate without soiling it.

By eleven they'd done all that might reasonably be done. Nothing remained but to wait and watch and hope. Maggie Ryan, who was eighty-one, brought out a tray of coffee mugs, and another with sandwiches. They ate them in silence. By noon, the waters began to accumulate about the storm-drains and the verges. Slowly, a reflective sheen spread over the roads and the common. Word was that somewhere near the boat club, a wall had subsided. Once the water began to climb their rampart of sandbags, they handed out an arsenal of spades and yard-brushes, of buckets and containers with which to bail. There sounded the indefatigable chug of a water-pump on loan from a building-site that coughed gouts of yellow seepage back into the flood.

The level continued to inch up. Outside the dyke, a vast drab tide was drifting endlessly south.

Still they hoped.

When the blow fell, it sickened like a betrayal. A literal stab in the back. Maggie Ryan, whose house was on the lowest ground, stumbled from her doorway, deploring what was just then sobbing up over her toilet-bowl. They ran to look, and saw that the floor was awash. One after another, the houses succumbed. Liquid, oily and foul-smelling, surged up through the drains and outlets with a hydraulic logic they could no longer counter. It was neither as deep nor as precarious as the first flood, but even as the bulwark of sandbags held and the main danger passed, the entire terrace was infiltrated with an ankle-deep, rust-coloured slick infected with sewage. Even the men broke down.

It took several months before Clodagh consented to move back. Kyle had installed himself in an upstairs bedroom, throwing himself vociferously into a new lawsuit to nail 'that son-of-a-bitch that built the estate on a goddamn floodplain, for Christ-sakes.' She knew as well as he that this crusade was to compensate for the fall-off in work, now that his company was downsizing; for his lack of foresight in refusing flood cover; for his unforgiveable absence in the face of the enemy. Having lived there ten weeks he'd cleared out the ground floor and had it decontaminated, but little else. It remained cold, and musty, and entirely bare.

'Where's Becky?' he'd asked. 'She's not with you?'

'I'm leaving her with Dee,' she said. And that was that. Until such time as the place could be called a home, that's where their child would remain. Looking at their bedroom, strewn with mounds of papers, with a jumble of his laundry behind the door and even several plates and pizza boxes, she added 'I'm moving into Becky's room.'

Having Kyle about the place made Clodagh realise how much she'd appreciated his absences over the previous few years. At first she felt constrained, as though she were constantly being watched. Soon, though, in their uneasy truce, it was tacitly understood that the restoration of the ground floor was her domain; his business was to shore up the support of the estate in the pursuit of communal legal redress. To be fair to him, he was tireless in this. When, as early as the second evening, she'd mentioned over a glass of wine 'you do know the developer filed for bankruptcy two years ago,' he'd sat back for a minute, shuffled a few thoughts, and declared 'then we'll go after the councillors, and that cowboy architect, and the whatchacallem civil engineers and whatever other sons-of-bitches signed off on this disaster-zone in the first place.'

She painted. She papered. She scraped. She sought out bargains. But with little of the zeal that had marked her first mission. There was an oppressive weariness about the entire estate it was difficult to escape. A number of For Sale signs mouldered over the course of that year. Maggie Ryan's house was boarded up, and word was she'd moved into a retirement home. With Becky in Dublin and Kyle on half-salary, Clodagh began to look for part-time work. It was fortunate that substitute teaching, when she could find it, paid reasonably well. They'd fallen several months into arrears, but no more than anyone else on the estate. She saw Becky every weekend, but rarely during the week. She even consented to Dee enrolling her in a school with special needs, somewhere in Cabra.

One day, looking over her work – the house was passably inhabitable, but to her eye a show-house, no more – she tapped at the door of their former bedroom. 'I think we should sell,' she told him.

'Sell? How?'

'This is no life, Kyle.' The lack of fight in her own voice surprised her. 'It's not even a home anymore.'

He stood. He removed the glasses he'd begun to wear and paced as far as the window. With his back to her and his hands in his pockets he examined the view, then slowly shook his head.

'So what are you saying? We wait around for the next big rain, is that it?'

He sighed. Again he shook his head. 'There's three, no, four For Sale signs on this street alone, or hadn't you noticed?'

'So what do you propose?'

'What I propose…,' he turned. In the look he fired her, something akin to animosity flared. His glasses back on he began to shuffle through a stack of papers. 'Ok, so what? We sell up? That your big idea?' Unable to locate the bank-statements he required, he slapped the bundle. 'Clodagh.' Deep breath. 'So this place sells for what? Hundred-fifty, hundred-sixty tops. That's saying we can find some chump dumb enough to take it on, which is by no means certain. Know what that means?'

'No, Kyle. What does that mean?'

'That means, my love, we walk outta here not just with Jack shit, not just with no roof over our heads, but with a legacy debt of a hundred, a hundred-ten grand. See what I'm saying? Take ten years just to clear that sort of figure. I mean, do the math. We're stuck with this, baby.'

A shiver racked her. That's twice already you fucked up, she thought, you do the math. She looked long at the man, unable even to bring him into focus.

As though it were the third term in a diminishing geometric progression, the next event arrived after an interval of two years. Once again, there was plenty of warning from the Met Office. Hard-hatted men in luminous jackets arrived with their trucks and diggers and sandbags. Clodagh didn't wait around to watch. She took the bus to Dublin, turned down the offer of the camp-bed in the spare-room where Becky had been sleeping, and installed herself on Dee's sofa. Kyle could stay on and play at sandcastles for all that she cared anymore.

Three days later, on foot of the inevitable news reports, Clodagh removed the house-key from the keyring and laid it flat on the breakfast table. 'Borrow an envelope?'

Dee shook her head. 'You're going to go through with it?'

'Yup.'

'But what will you do?'

She shrugged, feeling weightless. To have finally lost is a relief when one has been perpetually losing. 'Don't worry. I know we can't stay here,' she supplied, sticking her tongue out at Becky.

'That's not what I'm asking, Clo.' Dee lifted the key as if it was an artefact from an archaeological dig. 'I mean, what about Mam's money?'

'The deposit? My dear, that is well and truly lost.'

'So you'll what? File for bankruptcy, is it?' To fracture the surface of Clodagh's flippancy, Dee slapped the key back onto the table. 'Have you any idea what that would mean?'

'You're the financial expert.' Briefly, she frowned. 'People make out.' Then, to Becky, 'We'll be fine, won't we sweetie?'

Deirdre wasn't one bit convinced by the display. Her sister was being far too facetious. 'Ok. So what about Kyle?'

'He'll be in a hotel somewhere. The place is knee-deep in water.'

'But I mean… after.'

'It's my house, Dee. The deeds are in my name.' Becky had come to her, burrowed her forehead into her shoulder. 'Kyle Bradley has no interest in custody, believe me.' She wondered if Becky knew; a wise child. She placed a palm on the soft hair. 'You'll stay up here with Auntie Dee. Won't you Becks?'

At least Dee had no inkling. 'And if he phones?'

Clodagh lit a cigarette. Already she could hear the weir's incessant churn. The thrill of vertigo; of letting go.

'Tell him…' She blew an orchid of smoke into the air, as all the disdain that had accumulated for seven years concentrated in her features. 'Tell him the goddamn word is maths.'

Half-A-Boy - Fiction by Anne Walsh Donnelly

"Mattie, stop. You'll burn the house down," said Mam, prodding me in the back with the poker, the other day.

But there's no heat in the sods anymore, no matter how many I put on the fire and now I'm kicking huge holes in the bank those sods came out of.
"Useless fucking turf."

Maybe it's Grey I should be kicking? For throwing Joe off his back the last time we were going to the bog. Or that big lump of a stone that hit Joe in the head when he fell. Bloody stones. We'd killed ourselves half the summer picking them out of the top field and they still came back. I reckon God does make it rain stones in the middle of the night. He must think we haven't much to be doing except picking stones. But He's wrong; we've lots to be doing.

Joe's in hospital now. The grey brick one on the edge of Castletown. St. Bridget's. That's why I'm walking through the bog. I'm going to see him and it's much quicker to go the bog-way. I want him to come home before everything falls apart. Sure I wouldn't be here, to save turf in the middle of November, would I?

I wish I was, saving turf, meself and Joe. We used to have great craic, we did. Jumping off the banks as we swigged tea from whiskey bottles and taking huge chunks out of Mam's soda bread.

"Time for ye to stop being so wild. Ye're nearly men now."

Mam's killed telling us that.

"Old enough to start acting responsibly."

"What does she mean, Joe?"

"We have to stop messing, that's what she means."

I'd do me best to stop messing if he'd come home from hospital. I would.

She got rightly riled the day he fell off Grey. Said it was my fault. If I wasn't cod-acting the horse wouldn't have bolted but that's not the way it was at all. If she'd let me explain I'd have told her that. But no, she believed Fr. Constantine. It was him striding down the lane lifting his bat-wing cassock so it wouldn't dip into the cow shite. That's what frightened old Grey. I'm sure of it.

I was walking alongside the horse with the turf spades in me hands and when I saw Fr. Constantine me fingers let go off them.

"Waving the spades over his head, he was. No wonder the horse jumped," he said to Mam.

I don't remember doing that. All I remember is the blood, splattered all over that stony field and me bawling 'cos I thought Joe was dead on account of him looking so pale.

I'm shivering now and I know I wouldn't be shivering if Joe was here. How long does it take to fix him up?

"Just a bang to the head. He'll be right in no time," said Mam, when she came home from the hospital.

81

So why is he still there? And anyway St. Bridget's not a real hospital; everyone knows that it's not. They don't keep you long in real hospitals; weeks at the most not months. And it's months he's there and every time I see him it's worse he seems to be getting. He'll hardly talk or make a grunt or anything and his face is all crooked.

"It's the tablets he's on." Mam says. "He needs them for those awful headaches he gets."

It's them tablets that have him the way he is but I can't say that or me cheek will be stinging from the flat of her fingers. And I can't do things as good as he used to. The cows won't stop kicking when I'm trying to milk them. It's me hands. Sure what cow wouldn't kick a buck with cold hands?

So I decided today seen as it's a Sunday and Mam's gone to Mass, I'd go see Joe.

"He has my poor heart broken. He won't even go to Mass anymore. Will you talk to him?" she said to Fr. Constantine last week.

Then she told him what I did to the picture of Jesus and the two robbers on the crosses that's on our bedroom wall. He did talk to me and I told him.

"It's their eyes. They won't stop looking at me when I'm trying to sleep and it wasn't so bad when Joe was in the bed beside me. Some nights when I couldn't sleep he'd throw his shirt over the picture so the two robbers couldn't look at me. But Joe wasn't there the other night nor was his shirt. So I took his ash stick from under the bed, the one he plays hurling with and smashed the picture only to stop those two robbers looking at me, Father."

Of course that's not really true. Joe was in one of me dreams and he told me to smash that bloody picture 'cos he hates the sight of Christ after Him letting *him* fall off Grey. But I couldn't tell the priest that.

Jesus, I have me shoes destroyed from kicking that turf bank. Mam'll kill me if she sees the state of them. Well, no point in trying to clean them now, not till I get out of the bog anyway. There's a fierce black cloud in the sky. I'd better hurry up or I'll get soaked and they mightn't let me past that big green door in St. Bridget's with wet clothes and mucky shoes. Maybe I shouldn't have gone this way at all.

"Would you just stop and think before you do something?"

That's what Mam is always saying.

"He wasn't made for thinking. I do the thinking, he does the doing," Joe used to say.

Then he'd knock Dad's old peak cap off me head, put his hand under me chin and lift me face to make sure I was listening.

"Isn't that right, Mattie?"

But I'm *thinking* now, 'cos Joe's not here to do it for me. And I'm thinking I'm not much use to Mam without him around. And I'm remembering what Fr. Constantine said to her last night;

"Would you consider putting Mattie in St. Bridget's? They'll take him now he's eighteen."

"I don't know if I could bear having the two of them in there," she said.

"He's no use to you here and if he can destroy a picture of Our Lord there's no telling what he might do to you."

"But that was only because he was so upset about Joe and I need a man to work the farm."

"I hate to say this to you, but Mattie will never be a man. He's only half-a-boy, God bless him. You could sell the land."

I wanted to shout:

"Isn't half-a-boy better than no boy?"

But I couldn't 'cos then they'd know I was hiding behind the couch and there'd be fierce trouble altogether.

"Paddy would turn in his grave if I let the farm go."

Me Dad turning in his grave didn't seem to bother Fr. Constantine.

"It'd still be in the family if you sold it to your brother-in-law. I'm looking for a housekeeper. That'd be a much easier life for you."

I know I'd be with Joe if they put me in St. Bridget's but I can't stand the smell there. I do hold me nose when I go to see him but I couldn't be doing that for the rest of me life. And once they'd put me in I might never get out. And it's not as if they'd let me sleep with Joe. The matron told me to shush the last time I was there.

"You're upsetting the other patients. They don't like loud noise," she said.

I was only trying to tell Joe about the fox taking the hens and me running after him with Dad's shotgun. Fr. Constantine took that too.

And there'd be no jumping on beds or anything like that. All the men in Joe's ward do is drag their legs after them and you should see the big humps of shoulders on them. When you try to talk to them, they'll either keep looking at the floor or else look right through you, as if you weren't standing there in front of them. And the worst thing of all is I don't think Joe knows me. He won't even smile when he sees me coming and if he doesn't know me sure how can I get him to come home with me?

There's the quarry. I wasn't long getting through the bog after all. I'll get some grass and take the muck off me shoes before I go out to the road. The lake on the floor of the quarry looks awful oily. I wonder what'd be like in there now. Maybe I'd turn into an eel if I dived in. We had one for tea once. Joe caught it in the River Barrow and it was a Friday. You should have seen it jump all over the pan while Mam was trying to cook it. And as for the taste of it.

I know that lake's quare deep 'cos Joe tried to dive to the bottom of it one day when I threw in a penny that Fr. Constantine gave me on one of his visits. But I couldn't stand the church smell that was on it. You know the smell you get when they wave that thing around at Mass and smoke comes out of it. Fr. Constantine waved it around Dad's coffin and I nearly got sick right there in the front seat of the chapel. But I swallowed it back down again 'cos I knew that I'd get a clip around the ear if me porridge came up and landed all over Fr. Constantine's shiny black shoes.

"There's no bottom in that lake." Joe said. "That penny's gone straight to hell."

"I wouldn't go to hell. Would I, Joe?"

"No, boys like you go straight to heaven."

The muck won't come off me shoes. No point in going to town in dirty shoes and if I go home Mam'll surely kill me when she sees them or worse, march me straight into St. Bridget's in me bare feet.

Maybe half-a-boy isn't better than no boy.

What'll I do then? I'll climb our tree, that's what I'll do. Though it looks awful sad, bent over as if it's about to jump into the quarry. I love the leaves on it. They have five fingers. But there's no leaves on it today, they're all on the ground and they're the colour of calf scour.

Joe used to hang a rope off one of the branches and we'd swing out over the quarry's edge, roaring our heads off and he'd shout at me:

"Don't let go."

Ropes gone though. I can still climb it though. All the way to the top. Out onto the longest branch. Lying down hugging it I am and I wish it was Joe I was hugging.

"Let go."

"Why Joe?"

"You want to be free, don't you?"

I'm a monkey. Me arms and legs hanging on to the branch. See how long I can hang with just me arms and now - one hand. See if I can count to ten. The Master used to grip the cane fierce tight when I tried to count for him in school.

Close me eyes. Whatever happens; it'll be God's will, as Fr. Constantine says.

I'm a snipe. No. A hawk.

"Can you see me now, Joe?"

I'm wet and there's an eel with Joe's face and he wraps himself around one of me legs but I don't kick or wave or even breathe. And I'm not half-a-boy anymore. I'm an eel just like Joe and we swim round and round our oily lake.

The Art of Happiness – Fiction by Molly Fennig

The first kitten, Catalie Portman, lasts four days and six hours before you coax her into the crate and drive her back to Forever Friends Rescue. She stays silent, even when "Who Let The Dogs Out" blasts on the radio and you know it's another sign that she's not the right one, even though four days and six hours is the record, and Forever Friends says twenty three cats is too many to try out for adoption and maybe you should go somewhere else for the next one.

5B isn't any quieter without the ghost of a cat but it feels like it is—more empty and lifeless than normal. You take off your Yankees cap, run your fingers through uneven brown hair, pull sweatpants over ratty basketball shorts, letting out an exhale. Enough air for you and everyone not there, like Mom, probably at knitting club or doing power yoga, even though she hates both, because they're better than being in the ivy-covered brownstone on 155th in case Dad is there. And Dad, probably yelling at some intern about how not refilling the paper clips reflects a deep personality flaw and reveals her utter incompetence, not letting her squeak out that it was Hannah's turn that day. And Erin, oh Erin. You hope she is thinking of you, wondering where you are, pink iPhone in her hand, about to text you, beg you to come back to her.

The biting wind and February frost almost convince you to curl up on the bed, sleep through another Sunday, wrapped up in fuzzy blankets and Snickers wrappers, but you know your therapist Jenna will know you skipped coming in because it was a Bad Day, not because you had to go to brunch or the dentist or Zimbabwe. She'll tell you, again, that socializing and leaving the house are the best ways to Actively Fight and Distract Yourself and Feel Better. You don't understand how feeling numb outside is much better than feeling numb in bed, warm and cosy.

You remember the first day you went into her office, through halls made of glass, spending six and a half minutes walking to the door, reaching your hand out, dropping it, and stepping away. Finally going in after the short girl with dark braids and purple lips. Sitting on the waiting room couch that was so plush you sunk down and couldn't have left even if you changed your mind, which you were sure you were about to. Following the tall, blonde Jenna into the small beige room with a bookcase, a low, black couch facing two windows, and a single, orange chair.

She tells you it's normal to be lonely, but that most people occasionally have other emotions. You say you do have other emotions. She says sadness doesn't count. You don't say anything. Because neither Prozac, or Parnate, or Cymbalta, or Paxil, or the Elavil worked and most left you awake, staring at the ceiling as the clock ticked 2, 3, 5 am, dizzy and headachy. Gaining weight. Feeling guilty all the time because you couldn't get out of bed, didn't want to do anything but sleep, not even watch TV which was saturated with too much romance that sent you into thoughts about Erin and every mistake you made, every perfect moment together, the weight of missing her pushing tears and sobs out of you until you hyperventilate, heart pounding, can't breathe, why can't you breathe, what if this is your last breath and no one finds you for days and oh my gosh you're going to die, can't breathe, can't breathe, can't breathe.

Jenna asks about Catalie Portman. Suggests you try another cat. Reminds you to exercise, eat healthy. You feel the comforting weight of the Snickers bar in your jacket pocket, can't wait for the 55-minute session to be over so you can sink your teeth into it. Decide that maybe 23 cats mean the cats aren't the problem and maybe they aren't the cure you're looking for. Jenna asks for the Happy List where you're supposed to write down all the things that you appreciate, that make you happy.

1. Fuzzy blankets when the apartment gets chilly at night 2. Homemade Oreo Cupcakes (you don't write down that you ate all 12 in one sitting) 3. Sleep 4. Blue flowers in the window display on 96th 5. Not having to live with Dad anymore. Five for one week is a lot, at least for you, even though Jenna doesn't count sleep since it's an "un-activity". As you reach the 50th minute, Jenna asks you to try for 6 next week, to do at least two things besides going to work and getting groceries and looking at cats.

When you get back to the apartment you microwave a cup of macaroni, eat it sitting on the white marble countertop, The Great British Bake Off on in the background until you've finished, and the remaining pasta is cold, and you've been staring at the bubbling blue paint above the stove for so long your eyes sting from dryness.

You move to the plain, green couch in the living room that is only slightly more forgiving than the floor. Stare at the bookshelf that takes up an entire wall. Art and art history and art theory and the rest random, old library books you bought because you felt like you should have more, and they were only a dollar each, maybe two, and you think the smell alone is worth it. Stare at the ceiling fan that starts on its own. Don't get up to turn it off when it does, just watch the dusty, white blades spin around and around and around and lift the top sheet of the empty easel in the corner whose paint brushes you threw away one Saturday in May.

It only takes you three hours to fall asleep that night and you arrive at work a mere twenty minutes late. Your boss, Gerald, says nothing, just tightens his pink checkered tie and pushes his wire rim glasses farther onto his face, like he always has since you dropped the orange bottle one Thursday and he picked it up, read Zoloft, handed it back. You do decent enough work and don't cause too much trouble and with the number of college grads with advertising degrees declining it's not worth searching for someone to replace you. You could quit, too, but you've read enough pamphlets and self-help books to know big life decisions like that shouldn't be made during a depressive episode, so you're probably never going to work anywhere else.

You wish you knew before you got the job, armed with an art major and $2000, the latter being the more useful of the two, that Co-Assistant Art Director at Reach Agency was code for thousands-of-boring-odd-jobs-where-the-most-exciting-is-deleting-spam-email rather than stepping-stone-to-being-a-famous-artist-or-at-least-someone-who-doesn't-spend-half-the-day-looking-for-ways-to-skip-work-tomorrow. Jenna says it's good to hate work, or at least to have hate as an emotion. You say it's not hate so much as indifference. Jenna doesn't say anything.

After work you stop at Fur-ever Homes shelter, not because you want to be out of the house, nor have the 24th cat not work out, but because you don't want to have to spend so much time in the silent apartment. A large lady with a pink ruffled shirt, caked on blush, and a pushed-in pug nose leads you back. Most of the cats are easy to walk past, except one, Fuzz Aldrin. 8 months. Fluffy grey the color of your dog growing up who succumbed to cancer because he was exhausted by trying to keep you happy and safe but there were too many tears to lick off. Too many dinners sprinkled with stale silence, a cup of contempt. Too many people yelling and sharp words that shattered inside you, too far down to be fixed by a cuddle, a game of fetch. You leave without Fuzz even though he has everything you want from a cat and maybe, just maybe, he could make you smile.

You pick up the newspaper at the apartment entrance, recycle everything except the classifieds next to the elevator, scan it as the elevator ascends. Photographer wanted. Artist wanted. "Quit your job," it tells you. You recycle that section, too.

Since you know Jenna won't count The Great British Bake Off as one of the two weekly activities, you decide to make brownies. Dark chocolate with chocolate chips, the kind Mom used to bring to church and to potlucks as proof that you were one of those normal families that functioned enough to have time to bake.

Your phone buzzes. You drop the metal teaspoon when you see it's from Erin. *Hey. Do you still have my Harvard sweatshirt?*

You wonder what this is code for. I miss you and want you back? We never should have broken up? I still hate you? You also wonder if she knows you used to sleep with that sweatshirt every night, at least until it stopped smelling like her, detergent and warm salt water.

I think so

Cool, can I come get it? I'm in the city Saturday

Yeah, of course

As soon as you realize you've hit the send button, the floor gets shaky and you drop the mixing bowl which shatters into thousands of pieces and all you can think is *fuck.*

You pick up Fuzz Aldrin two hours later, just as the shelter is closing, just in case he can cure you by Saturday. He doesn't leave the plastic crate for thirty minutes, just stares at you in your polka dot boxers, tilts his head, wiggles his whiskers. Just as you think, *at least it'll be easier to take him back if he never gets out,* Fuzz stumbles onto the stained blue carpet.

At first he's quiet, like Catalie, just sitting on the foot of the queen bed and staring at you, eyes glowing in the dark, as you try to go to sleep. You roll over, trying not to feel him watching. A minute passes. A warm ball of fur spins in circles just below your bent knee, lies down.

And you learn what it's like to fall asleep on a pillow that is dry and unseasoned. No salt or sadness. Just a blanket of purrs, a few soft twitches. You almost feel rested when your alarm goes off, the sun peeling back the darkness.

Fuzz is still sleeping when you slip out the front door, but you leave a bowl of what he will consider a delicacy and what you consider mush. When you go to the kitchen for burnt, over-brewed coffee at lunchtime, you say hi to Bri in HR instead of lowering your head and studying the peeling laminate tiles like you usually do. She smiles, and you wonder if happiness would have the same shine as her eyes.

Gerald lets you leave half an hour early, perhaps as a reward for showing up on time, so you take the B and walk nineteen minutes to the Metropolitan Museum of Art where you spend twenty minutes in front of *Madonna and Child* by Duccio, wondering if you could have painted something remotely similar had you not given up your paint brushes for a nine-to-five black suit. You write the museum in your journal as one of the weekly activities, add *getting off work early* to the list of good things, and make your way back towards the subway.

Past the woman in athleisure holding twins, one strapped to her front, one to her back. Past the couple holding hands, despite the icy wind, the woman's dark, curly hair peeking out from a purple hat. Past the man in a trench coat over a blue suit, hair slicked back, phone to his ear, briefcase in one hand.

You have almost forgotten why you stopped coming to the Met and getting off at 81st street but the crooked shutters high above the street have not forgotten. Have not forgotten the stillness, Erin's coconut shampoo, her lips. Goodnight, whispered, a question. An invitation. One year and sixteen days later, a fact.

The shutters remind you, in whispers, all the way home. Past 69th and 116th, up the narrow sidewalk broken up by squares of dirt sprouting dead trees, tufts of grass, up five floors in the jerking elevator. Through the doorway where Fuzz sits, head still turned slightly to the right, admiring the pile of smashed cups on the hardwood in front of him.

The one you bought when you and Erin went to DC in March with a black and white picture of the Washington monument that you liked, and she thought was overly dramatic. The blue one printed with Starry Night that she gave to you on your birthday along with a bottle of whiskey and dinner at Eso.

Fuzz looks at you, proud of the mess, and you wonder how he knew to only break those three. You give him an extra big scoop of mush, scratch him behind the ears, throw away the fragments of what used to be your life.

Mom calls at seven because Tuesdays are golf nights and Dad won't be home, not that him being there or not changes how she talks. "How are you?" she asks, which is code for, "should I be worried?" and "are you feeling suicidal?" and, because you've had this conversation more than any other, you know to reply, "doing well" which means "doing poorly, but not enough to burden you with it more than you already worry, although I'm not sure if you do worry because we never really talk about it." You mention that Gerald let you off early for good behavior and she mentions that Becky from yoga invited her for cocktails and you both agree those are great things, how great it is that you are doing so great, and promise to talk again soon.

You lay on the bed, diagonally because you don't get to—have to—share it with anyone, and watch the clock count to sixty, three times, and even then, you don't have the strength to sit up, nonetheless stand, nonetheless try to quiet the voices and the memories and the numbness long enough to go to sleep.

Fuzz yelps and you hear a crash so you force yourself up. You grab the grey fleece blanket and tie it around your neck like a cape as you run into the living room. The easel is on its side and the last piece you were working on, a field of flowers, has escaped and sits in the middle of the floor.

The colors are still all wrong, the greens not yellow enough, the blues too purple. You had forgotten about this painting since you stuffed it behind the sketchpad after hours of mixing and remixing paint, never quite getting it right.

You pick up the easel, place the canvas back in front, and pick up a dusty brush from the shelf. Squirt paint onto a plastic palette and get hypnotized by the swirls of the brush bringing new shades to life. Fuzz climbs up the bookshelf until he is at eye level and sits, cocking his tiny head to one side as you stir. Your brush leaves a trail in the sky, the vibrant blue it had been hoping for. After that, you mix in more white and sponge on clouds and realize you don't remember the last time you were outside and looked up.

You also realize it is dark and you will have to remember to look when you go out to give the sweatshirt back tomorrow. When you look at the clock you realize it is past midnight.

You stand up. In the kitchen sink the brush bleeds blue. It dyes the water and the soap as you knead the bristles between your fingers. You put water in a mason jar. You don't know why you even have mason jars except you feel like it is something people with apartments have.

This time you mix yellow and green and dots of other colors until you have a vibrant grass which you apply in swift strokes. Fuzz knocks over the water with one swipe of his paw.

You set the brush down to get paper towels. You clean up the blots of lightly tinted water, and pull the bookshelf over to cover up the rest. On your way back from the trash can, you stop. You sit in the old lounge chair across the room and your eyes scan the painting and you realize you maybe really like it. The contrasting of the blue and the green and the way you can focus on the brush strokes or the whole scene and either way you feel breathless.

You check your phone. 3 am. Fuzz is curled up on the window sill, asleep. You find another canvas and place it on the easel and get out another palate.

You text Erin, *can't do tomorrow. can't find your sweatshirt*

And you put the ragged thing in the musty hall closet, in the bottom of the blue, plastic bin to be hauled away to Goodwill or ThreadUp, tomorrow or the next day or the day after, and add Fuzz to the list of good things along with acrylic paint and blank canvases.

"I remember you," the stranger sang, back handling the door, and ringing the hanging bells between the lyrics in Peggy's head.

Peggy looked up from the compass she was repairing. It had gotten wet and the needle was rusty. The pin was stuck. It would need to be re-magnetised. She had a large magnet that would spin the needle north in a few seconds. It was an easy fix. Fifteen to twenty minutes at most. She had repaired dozens over the years. She had been using a flat screwdriver to remove the glass from an overlap of copper casing that had been dinted in around it. She was half way around when the door swung wide open.

"You don't remember, do you?" He asked, stepping forward into the dark light of the antique shop. It was that kind of day where the sun dipped in and out from the clouds, so all the lights had to be left on for the darker moments. The sunlight and hanging streams of raw bulbs above the counter transformed every customer into a faceless form in motion.

"I remember they were stringing the Christmas lights around you, making you light up like an angel. You were only sixteen years of age at the time. Sweet Sixteen. A sight for sore eyes, you were. You still are. If only I was back there now."

His words were quick, but he was walking a slow step towards her. He might even have been older than herself. He had definitely left sixty years behind him.

She finished pressing down around the full circle of the small case by the time his toes touched the bottom of the counter. She expected the glass to pop out, but it was thick and stubborn. A blade was needed to ease it out. She plucked one from the work bench behind her and began pressing the blunt blade gently into the case, careful not to damage the glass.

"The school party," he said.

She felt the seal breaking. She could feel the glass easing forward, craving to pop out from the case's grizzly rusty clutch. Any moment now it would drop out and she would catch the small round glass piece on the coarse pads of her fingers. She looked at the stranger's face, trying to remember Christmas lights being wrapped around her. She shook her head and searched his face for any twitch that might trigger her memory. Nothing.

"You started working in this shop Christmas week. You broke more than you fixed. I never enjoyed anyone breaking things as much. It didn't take you long to learn. Your mind was a deep well waiting for water." He laughed, but his laughter could have been mistaken for crying. It was carrying the weight of watchful restraint.

"Did you work in the shop too?" Her mind raced through all the people who had worked alongside her over the years.

"We couldn't get you out of the shop when you got the hang of it. Billy Finbarr was your only distraction." His voice reached down into his chest and stayed there at the mention of the boy's name.

"Billy Finbarr," he repeated, clearing his throat, "do you remember him?"

She smiled at him and the image of the compass transformed into Billy's flirty smirky face. He had discarded her so easily when a new girl came to live in the town. Nothing but trouble that Billy Finbarr, her mother used to say. Billy used to say that Peggy was working backwards because she was repairing things that had no use or relevance to the world any more. He wore the latest fashions, listened to the latest records, and spoke the latest slang. Nothing was old about Billy. He replaced his girlfriends with newer, more modern versions at every opportunity. Still, he must be old himself now, she thought.

"You haven't changed that much since then. You're still preoccupied with those old objects, aren't you?" His words slid in between the pictures of her memories.

Peggy spent her days restoring old objects to what might have been if they hadn't been tarnished, cast aside, or lost. The presence of dust excited her. It was a cover to lift off the past and bring back all its good. Dust encased treasures in sticky webs of mildew, mould, and dirt. The stories that could possibly lie behind each reworked item were endless. She preoccupied herself with cleaning, repairing and displaying; each object brought her back to where everything did what it was supposed to do, and nothing needed fixing anymore.

"I'm sorry, your name is just not coming to me at the moment," she said, shaking her head and smiling politely.

She flicked the back of the case to encourage it out. A sliver slipped out. It was almost there. A couple more flicks and it should release itself. There. It popped out as if it was never stuck. She placed the dirty glass on the counter and shook out the rusty pin into her curved hand.

"It was a long time ago." He looked down at her hands at work. They never stopped for thought. They were busy bees with an important job to finish, automatic in their movements, meticulous in their application, and as steady as they had been in their prime.

"It must have been. Aren't you going to tell me your name? It'll surely come back to me then."

"Sandpaper and coke for that," he said, pointing at her left hand. He stared at her wedding ring and sighed.

"Well you seem to know your way around repairing a compass, if you'll excuse the pun," she said, scrapping the less visible side of the pin against the sandpaper to flatten it.

"I'll just have a look around the shop." He tapped on the counter softly and walked deeper into the middle of the antique stock for sale in the shop.

Peggy frowned at him and wondered why he wouldn't tell her his name. She thought she might remember who he was by the time he was finished browsing. She dropped the pin into a glass of coke once she had flattened it as much as was possible with the sandpaper. She cleaned the glass in a small dish of soapy water, dried it, and placed it beside the glass of bubbling rusty coke. Soon it would be pristine too.

She raised her head to look at the stranger again. She examined his outline and watched him lift small objects, inspecting each one closely with his eyes, questioning their past purpose and owner.

His gait seemed familiar. It was comforting to look at. He didn't appear out of place, like many customers do in a shop full of antiques from other worlds and times. He lifted each item confidently, like he had lifted them before, like he knew where they had come from, like they were his own. She shook her head. She couldn't place him.

91

Her eyes returned to the bubbling coke. Onto the magnet. She dried the pin and inserted it back into its base plate, covering it with its glass cover. She rubbed the magnet back and forth over the compass, slowly from south to north and back again, trying to remember the memory the stranger had of her at sixteen years of age. The compass soon found north, and she returned the magnet to the furthest end of the workbench behind her. The compass was fixed. She didn't want to demagnetise it. It was ready to orient somebody, maybe for an adventure of a lifetime.

"I'm sorry. That memory seems to be gone. It's a lot of Christmases since I was sixteen." The stranger smiled as he approached the counter, this time with a red plate in his hands.

"A memory is always with us, even if we forget. Significant emotions are never forgotten. Something will remind us how the memory made us feel and then we'll remember. Always happens." The stranger put the plate down beside the compass. The little compass looked insignificant compared to the vibrancy of the large red plate.

"History never forgets, even when nobody records it." He circled the dust into his fingertips to reveal a shade of light red.

"Fascinating. I'm sure I'll remember so." She thought how arrogant he was to suppose that a moment was significant for her just because he remembered it.

"It's a bit dusty, but the red is like a ruby, don't you think?" The stranger guided Peggy's eyes back down to the plate.

"My daughter's name is Ruby," she said, picking up the plate to examine the extent of the dust.

"I'll clean that right up for you, but you will have to tell me your name first. You're a bit of a mystery now."

"My wife insisted we have a set of red dining plates when we moved into our first house. They weren't too different from these ones. It's a pity there isn't a full set. I'd love to have them again, for old time's sake. You know?"

"I do. Did the others break then?"

"They did. One by one until there was only one remaining."

"Oh, what a pity. Well now you'll have two."

Peggy rubbed the heavy dust off the plate with a cloth. It was made of fine bone china. The squiggly lines around the rim seemed to spread out in random directions, like tree roots reaching out for space to grow.

She thought back to her school days when she longed for freedom; to stretch her limbs so that she would appear more grown-up; to stretch her legs beyond the boundaries of the town to explore whatever the rest of the world offered.

She felt sorrow and excitement in her stomach - two conflicting feelings that didn't make sense to her. She rubbed her stomach as if she could rub them away.

"Gerry Tomalin," she said, clapping the dust off between her hands.

"Gerry Tomalin," she repeated, sticking her thumbs into her hips.

The boy who got the girl in trouble, she thought.

"I remember you. We went to school together. How could I forget? You used to work in the shop too, yes that's right. I remember," she said, looking at her husband with stranger's eyes.

"What brings you back into town?" She turned her back on him to walk over to the sink behind the workbench. A quick dip in soapy water was all this plate needed to restore its shine. She turned on the tap, twisted herself around and waited for Gerry's reply. Her daughter appeared in the doorway of the storeroom just as she was about to speak to him again.

"Ruby," she shouted, "this is Gerry Tomalin, an old friend from school. Can you believe it?"

Gerry Tomalin is here, she heard her friend whisper in her mind as she placed a red string of Christmas lights around her shoulders. I love you, she heard Gerry say after she told him that Billy Finbarr made her pregnant. Gerry Tomalin, I love you, she heard herself say, staring at his face through a veil at the local church altar. Do you take this man, Gerry Tomalin, for better for worse, in sickness and in health…she heard the priest ask. I do, she heard herself reply.

Gerry Tomalin, if you break one more of those plates…, she heard herself threaten, standing in their kitchen with one half of a broken ruby red plate, just like the one she was about to wash in the sink. We'll call her Ruby, he said, looking down at their new-born baby.

"Gerry," she whispered. Her hands turned off the tap and she walked back over to the counter to face her husband.

"I fixed the compass." She smiled at him the way she did when she was sixteen.

"See?" She shook it and let the pin find its way back to north.

The third time the beach ball hit the roof, Kurt sprang from his deckchair and yelled at the culprits, shaking his fist like Popeye the sailor.

'Well honestly,' he muttered under his breath as he sank back into the low chair next to mine, under the nylon arc of the sun-shelter. He shook the sand off his newspaper and balanced it back on his leg, covering his ugly scar from where they had chopped out the tumor. I watched, jaws clenched, as the guys jeered and resumed their play, their oiled torsos gleaming in the midday sun. That was when I first saw her.

She was the whitest person on the beach. That was the first thing I noticed about her. She must have just arrived here, I thought. You can't stay that white for long in Sydney. I lost sight of her amongst the hordes and turned back to my book.

I must have dozed off because when I awoke, Kurt was missing. Then I spotted him, beyond the waves, his long, sinewy arms slapping out that unmistakable backstroke.

'Excuse me,' I heard a woman say. It was her, even paler close up. 'I'd like to go for a swim and I was wondering if you could mind my wallet? It's just…' She trailed off. 'I'm here on my own. I won't be long.'

American? I thought at first. *No, Irish*, I concluded from the lilt. She held the wallet like a nervous kid offering a carrot to a horse. I studied her appearance through the cover of my sunglasses. Classy one-piece swimsuit. Perfectly manicured toenails in a metallic hue. Peacock. That's what it was. A pretty face but with something in her expression I couldn't quite place. A delicate vein throbbed at her temple.

'Of course! Enjoy your swim,' I said, taking the wallet. There was more than gratitude in her smile. I sensed something like relief in the way her face opened up. As she walked away, I called after her, 'Take your time. We'll be here a while.'

Off she went, picking her way through the bright maze of towels and beach umbrellas. I turned my attention to the wallet. Patent leather. I could see my distorted reflection like in a funfair mirror— all garish mouth and sunglasses, no chin or forehead. It was heavy for its size. *Probably has her phone in there too.* I threw it on the other deckchair and retrieved my novel. It wasn't the page-turner the jacket had promised. Suddenly I felt hot and longed for a dip but now I'd have to wait for her to come back.

'You did *what*?' he asked, as he flapped the towel around his body. 'God knows when she'll be back. We're stuck here now.'

I bit my lip. As if that hadn't crossed my mind.

'It's called being part of a community,' I muttered, hoping he would lower his tone. 'You ever heard of that, Kurt? A good deed for a fellow human being? We'll be here for a while anyway,' I sighed. 'Sandwich?'

At least another hour passed before he finally spoke: '*Now* what?' I hated that look. That trademark expression of disdain he reserved for me. I snatched up the wallet and unzipped it. Surely there would be something in here that would tell us who she was or where she was staying.

'Sweet Jesus, Anna, who brings that kind of money to the *beach*?' Kurt was gaping at the wallet. It took me a few seconds to register that it was packed with crisp green banknotes. Nothing useful, like a driver's license or a hotel room key. I put it under my seat. I felt angry and I wasn't even sure with whom. How bloody inconsiderate. Where the hell could she *be*?

I stared at the water for some time, hypnotised by the never-ending procession of waves—building, cresting, breaking. The surfers looked tiny against them. A scan of the beach yielded no sign of the woman. How bizarre that she hadn't returned. Gasping for a cool dip, I left him there, propped inside the sun tent, safe from the ultra-violet rays that now frightened him.

Pretty rough today, I thought, as I bobbed in the safety of the enclosed rock pool. Floating on my back, I let go, feeling the water absolve me. That's when I heard the helicopter droning overhead. Opening an eye to the salt and glare, I spotted it, mosquito-like, hovering above the beach. Faint alarm bells rang. A shark-sighting, perhaps? I had once heard of a reef shark being washed into a surf pool. I closed my eyes and floated a little longer, considering that scenario. Not the worst way to go. All over in a couple of minutes.

Kurt had dismantled the sun tent when I returned. *What did you do that for? She'll never find us now.* He was standing, talking with a broad-shouldered guy in a pair of board shorts.

'Looks like someone's snuffed it,' the guy was saying. 'A woman. Chopper's gonna bring her in.'

I glanced at my chair, untouched, the wallet still visible underneath. My stomach flipped. Oh God, where *was* she? Just a quick swim, she'd said. But that was hours ago.

'What are we going to do with this?' Kurt asked, picking up the wallet.

'We'll drop it off at the police station,' I said.

'No we won't,' he said. 'You know what they'll do? A wad of cash like that—are you kidding me?'

'What do you suggest?' I said. 'You want to stay here overnight in case she comes back in the morning? Why don't you sleep in your bloody tent?'

'Let's leave a note for her,' he said, indicating the information board that displayed water temperature, tides and stinger danger.

I snatched the wallet back and stomped off towards the notice board, leaving him staring after me. He was unused to such outbursts, my fury usually contained behind a veneer of compliance.

A crowd buzzed round the ambulance parked on the grassy strip overlooking the beach. Ghouls. Gossips. Seagulls around a chip. The helicopter had gone and the body now lay shrouded on a stretcher. I cringed at the idea of lurking, but I had to see her. All I could see as I edged through the mob was the soles of her feet protruding from the drape.

'Overseas tourist,' I could hear muttered.

'Couldn't handle the waves.'

'Outside the flags. Surfer spotted her.'

Another victim of Australia's less infamous killers. It always fascinated me how visitors would widen their eyes about funnel web spiders, great white sharks or saltwater crocs, when these accounted for so very few deaths each year. Fewer than deaths from dog attacks, I'd been told. Meanwhile they overlooked the real killers. The sun. The sea.

I was almost near enough to touch her when a policewoman planted a firm hand on my arm. 'I'm sorry madam, no civilians past this point.'

'But I must see her; I think I know who she is.' I pushed past her just enough to glimpse one foot a little better. Bunions—worse than my own. And her toenails—ugly, unpolished. Relief was replaced by a strange sense of disappointment. 'It's not her,' I said, as much to myself as the policewoman.

'You'll have to come with me, madam. If you have any information that can help us identify the body, you must tell us.'

'I'm telling you, it's not her,' I pleaded, but it was too late.

Kurt drove to the station, his lips pressed together in a hard line. 'It's not *my* fault we got a parking ticket,' I said as he floored it up the hill.

'Whose fault then, hmm? Whose fault that we have to spend half the bloody day on the beach because you want to do something for a complete stranger?'

The police station smelled of piney disinfectant and instant coffee and was hotter than the beach. *Imagine working here.* I was still crusted with salt and sand and dressed only in a sarong over my swimsuit. Kurt returned with his second cup of dire coffee. 'How can you drink that stuff?' I asked him.

He stared at me. 'You're not going to tell them about the wallet, are you?'

'Oh, for God's sake Kurt, the wallet's got nothing to do with the dead woman. That's just going to cause more confusion. I'm no use to them. Why can't they get that?'

As I lay between fresh bedsheets that night, after a long shower, I thought about how she'd looked, that Jane Doe, lying under the drape. Her body unclaimed. How *small* she had been at this critical point, the end of her tenure on earth. I didn't fear death but I never wanted to die like her. Alone. Unrecognised.

'Did you put the wallet somewhere safe, Anna?' said Kurt, his voice muffled by the pillows.

'Christ, Kurt. A woman drowned out there today and another woman is possibly missing and all you can think about is that fucking wallet. We can't just keep it,' I said, regretting that we hadn't given it to the police when we had the chance.

'We're just minding it until she contacts us,' he said. His voice had a zeal I recognised. He was spending it already, damn him.

Kurt shaved as I dressed for work the next morning, the steady *schip, schip* of the razor breaking the silence. He clipped his dark moustache and snipped at the hairs poking from his nostrils.

I surveyed the room reflected in the mirror as I fumbled with my earrings. How long had it been since this room had been a place to be held, to be nurtured? Halfway through strapping on my good watch, I stopped dead. I stared at the reflection of my arm. Now I remembered. The woman on the beach had worn the same one. The blue cabochon stone in the winder had glinted in the sun. This was not something you would wear into the sea. Ever. Where on earth had she gone? You can't just disappear. Can you?

Kurt was sitting on the bottom of the stairs tying his shoelaces when I stepped past him. 'I won't be back tonight,' he said. He was wearing his best tie and his shoes gleamed in the sunlight streaming through the hallway. I knew where he would be.

'Where did you put that wallet?' he asked, as I opened the front door.

'I've put it away,' I said. 'I'll get it for you later—when I get back from work.' I knew then that he would never get his hands on that wallet, or what was in it. I felt strangely protective of it, almost as though it were more than just an object. It was my connection to her, and perhaps to more. I would never spend a single cent from it, but at that moment it was worth to me a thousand times more than what it contained.

I loved this beach. We used to come here when the kids were little because it was safer than the surf beaches in Sydney. It was worth the drive then and it was worth it this bright morning.

I scrunched along the shoreline, sinking ankle deep in the fine gravel of tiny shells, some no bigger than a baby's fingernail. Millions of them.

Most people sat a little further back on the fine white sand that lured people from across the globe. The whitest sand in the world. I shielded my eyes from the blinding glare as I studied them. Stepping off the swathe of shells, I made for a nearby couple—tourists, judging by the depth and evenness of their tans. And their tattoos. Not many locals had tats around here.

I folded my sarong and placed it neatly on a rippled patch of sand and turned to them. I was hot from the walk and the patent leather felt slippery in my hand. 'Excuse me, would you mind looking after my wallet? I'm just going for a swim. I won't be long…'

They would later tell the police that I wore kingfisher nail polish on my toenails. But when they questioned the woman in the red suit at the car rental place, she'd get the colour right.

Reviews

Reviews Editor, Jane Simmons, looks at Denise Riley's: *Say Something Back*

Picador Poetry
ISBN 978 4472 7037 9

Denise Riley was born in Carlisle in 1948 and educated at Cambridge and Oxford. She is a critically acclaimed writer of both philosophy and poetry, and she is currently Professor of the History of Ideas and of Poetry at the University of East Anglia. She has also held a number of visiting positions: A.D.White Professor at Cornell University; Writer in Residence at the Tate Gallery; Visiting Fellow at Birkbeck College, University of London. She has taught in various academic fields – philosophy, art history, poetics, and creative writing – and written extensively on philosophy, feminism, lyric, and literary history. She has published the following collections of poetry: *Marxism for Infants* (1977); the volume *No Fee* (1979), with Wendy Mulford; *Dry Air* (1985); *Stair Spirit* (1992); *Mop Georgette* (1993); *Selected Poems* (2000); and *Say Something Back* (2016), which was nominated for a Forward Prize for Best Poetry Collection. Riley's nonfiction prose includes works such as *War in the Nursery: Theories of the Child and Mother* (1983); *'Am I That Name?': Feminism and the Category of Women in History* (1988); *The Words of Selves: Identification, Solidarity, Irony* (2000); and *Impersonal Passion: Language as Affect* (2005). Her chapbook, *Time Lived, Without Its Flow* (2012), is a meditation on time after the sudden death of a child. Linking poetry and prose, a sequence of 20 short poems from the chapbook, titled "A Part Song," was published in the *London Review of Books* and won a Forward Poetry Prize for Best Single Poem. Her most recent book is *Say Something Back* (Picador, 2016).

The collection *Say Something Back* takes as its starting point lines from W S Graham's *Implements in their Places*

Do not think you have to say
Anything back. But do you
Say something back which I
Hear by the way I speak to you.

before beginning the most important poem of the collection, *A Part Song*, about the death of the poet's adult son, Jacob. This lengthy poem in several parts becomes a moving account of loss and grief. It begins with the short but powerful poem, *Maybe; maybe not*

When I was a child I spoke as a thrush, I
thought as a clod, I understood as a stone,
but when I became a man I put away
plain things for lustrous, yet to this day
squat under hooves for kindness where

fetlocks stream with mud – shall I never
get it clear, down in the soily waters.

This poem places what is to follow firmly in a Christian context, with its echoes of Corinthians – and in the English literary tradition, with its use of William Blake's symbols of the clod and the pebble or stone. A later poem echoes a speech from Shakespeare's *King Lear*. However, although Riley places the poem in the literary tradition, she soon begins to question the nature and purpose of song, or the lyric poetry which she is writing,

You principle of song, what are you for now

The obvious answer would be that the purpose of the lyrical elegy is to console, and to provide solace to those who are grieving,

I can't get sold on reincarnating you

As those bloody 'gentle showers of rain'

Or in 'fields of ripening grain' – ooh

Anodyne.

To the poet, such conventional attempts at consolation are woefully inadequate. She wants her dead son's living *lighthearted presence*, to be

bodied forth

Straightforwardly

and nothing less than this will do.

Not only does she reject the idea of lyrical elegy, and its purpose of offering consolation, she also rejects the expected voice of lyric poetry. In an interview with Kevin Corcoran, Denise Riley spoke of the influence of song on her poetics:

Perhaps song in general is, in the end, purely 'for itself'. Whereas in 'A Part Song', its particular question was: what is the song for, in the teeth of this particular death. What can it do now? And what is its singer for, now? The only answer is: this instance of song is simply its own existence as voiced solidarity with the [not uncommon] experience of being left alive when your child isn't. But this solidarity lies in raising that question of what it's for, in concert with others' questioning, rather than in anything averred inside the poem itself. ... There's a universal impulse to ask, a need to know, however unlikely it is that any answer can appear; and here's just another instance of that usual impulse, still making its noise."

There is nothing quiet or reverent about the voice which the poet uses: the *I* of these lyric poems is a real mother, with a mother's scolding or reproachful tones. It is not formal, but informal, and very colloquial in its language and idiom. She is a *glum mum* or a *fat-lot-of-good mother*. This is what it makes it so powerful and moving - even painful - to read: the reader can hear the bereaved mother speaking to her dead son as if he is a living teenage boy

But by now

We're bored with our unproductive love,

And infinitely more bored by your staying dead

Which can hardly interest you much either.

She is unsparing in her comments and in her judgement of herself

Your dead don't want you lying flat

There'll soon be time enough for that

The reader is then witness to this intimate relationship – and the effect is that the characters live for the reader, as if they are real people and known personally. The picture which she presents of her son is not romanticised; she speaks of his *beaming* face, how he *lacked guile* and was *transparent*, but she also speaks of his *eczema scabs,* describes him as a *teen peacock,* and - in a moment of exasperation - calls him *a daft bugger.* Denise Riley's examination of her grief in *A Part Song* is unsentimental, never less than brave, and sometimes surprisingly witty.

The long, opening poem is a remarkable achievement - but it would be wrong to overlook the other poems in the collection. I have already referenced the echoes of Blake and Shakespeare in *A Part Song,* but this is not the only poem in the collection which positions itself in a literary tradition. In *Composed underneath Westminster Bridge*, Riley presents the reader with a contemporary companion piece to Wordsworth's earlier poem,

Broad gravel barges shove the drift. Each wake

Thwacks the stone steps. A rearing tug-boat streaked

Past moorhens dabbling floss, spun pinkish-beaked.

Peanuts in caramelised burnt chocolate bake

Through syrupy air. Above, fried onions cake.

Pigeons on steeleyed dates neck-wrestled, piqued.

Oblivious to their squabs that whined and squeaked

In iron-ringed nests, nursed in high struts. Opaque

Brown particles swarm churning through the tide

That navy hoop of cormorant can compose

A counter to this shield – eagles splayed wide,

Gold martlets – on the bridge's side; it glows

While through the eau-de-nil flaked arches slide

The boats 'Bert Prior' and 'The Eleanor Rose'.

In a poem which begins with lines from La Rochefoucauld, and considers how inanimate objects offer consolation *the light constancy/ of things.*

Her questioning of poetic forms, first seen in the questioning of the lyric in *A Part Song,* continues in the poem *Death makes dead metaphor revive.* In *Listening for Lost People,* the poet finds the dead in language itself

The souls of the dead are the spirit of language:

you hear them alight inside that spoken thought.

There are poems about the first world war and its enormous death toll – poems which continue her preoccupation with the subjects of animation and lifelessness, the living and the dead, the preoccupation which is the organising principle of this remarkable collection.

Emma Lee reviews *The Becoming of Lady Flambé* by Holly Magill

The Becoming of Lady Flambé
36 pages, £6.00 + P&P UK, ISBN 978-1-910834-86-2
Indigo Dreams Publishing

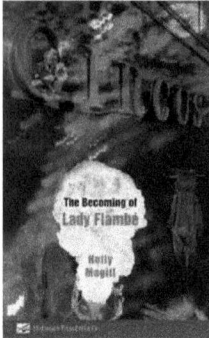

The Becoming of Lady Flambé takes readers to the circus and a liaison between an animal tamer and a bearded lady in "New arrivals" told from the viewpoint of Wayne, where Steve is a baby Asian elephant,

"Steve is awake - I need to get back, soothe him.

But the woman's eyes

seethe in the dark, will not let me

turn away. She waits

for me to draw near, much nearer

than I'd like, before she lets me

see the thing she cradles.

She had it, *Bella says*. And this one stays."

As the baby grows into a girl and as if being a redhead and unplanned wasn't enough, Steve becomes responsible for Lady Flambé's mangled foot and she develops ambivalence towards the elephant. It wasn't his fault but he left her disabled. She muses on Steve in "A whole lot of horse tranquilisers" after his death,

"No one will tell what they do with Steve's body;

would need an enormous hole to bury it,

like a crater on the moon.

There's jokes about an almighty hog-roast,

only not a hog - I'm going vegetarian.

We don't see the Ring Master for days;

empties fly from the windows of his trailer,

glass tears shatter on the hard-standing.

My ruined foot tingles. Wasn't me

that did it - but I wish I had."

The poem see-saws between a tenderness for the elephant and recognition of the hurt he caused. After initial disbelief there are the jokes, which Lady Flambé distances herself from, suggesting she doesn't hate the creature who injured her. She describes the Ring Master's grief, so is sensitive to the feelings of others, but she's also reminded that this creature damaged her. The key to her story is the lack of self-pity, which also comes through in "Things I learn",

"Juggling doesn't get you friends

at new schools. No one likes

a smart-arse.

How to - almost - be deaf

to yells of 'Pikey' and 'Gyppo'

and 'Cripple'.

Violet-satin eye-shadow is really pretty

on other girls.

Always smile at Social Workers;

it's not their fault.

Multi-tasking is easy - I can juggle and cry

at the same time, even in the dark."

A circus can't afford to have a member of its troupe sitting out and moping. There's a marriage, in "A small matter", where a "talkative Welshman called Leon" joins the circus and asks the Ring Master's permission, "a deal done behind red curtains." It's not successful as Leon is forced to leave and Lady Flambé banned from using knives. In the title poem, which is the last poem in the collection, readers see the disabled girl transform into performance,

"Legs stretched out - both feet bare

to the grass, the normal and the other.

People everywhere, people are smiling.

The tiny clay elephant tumbles loose

to my hand while I'm smirking badness

over those fried onions. A notch on its back

is threaded with a thin bootlace.

The creature is a small, warm weight

between my breasts as I gather

the tools of my trade:

103

matches, torches, accelerant, bananas.

I have everything I need to begin."

The collection successfully uses monologues. The speaker in each poem is clear and distinct. Use of colloquial phrasing is done to convey natural dynamics and give each speaker their own voice and viewpoint. It's a narrative sequence but each poem is capable of standing alone: Holly Magill has pulled off that balancing act of ensuring each poem can be read as a solo piece and also enabling each poem to slot into its narrative place and add to the overall story arc. "The Becoming of Lady Flambé" introduces dynamic, credible characters and grips readers' attention by deftly crafting a story through successful handling of multiple viewpoints. Like the best circuses, it takes its base material and transmutes into a quality performance.

The Theatrics of Privacy in an Age of Surveillance: Looking at the movie *Snowden* (2016) By - Simran Keshwani

Macquarie University

Introduction

History will recognize director Oliver Stone as one of the most important cinematic historians when it comes to the stories of his country, from Vietnam to Richard Nixon to 9/11 (Tallerico, 2016)

Oliver Stone's *Snowden* (2016) is a crisp portrait of the world's most celebrated whistle-blower. Reversing the usual pattern, it could be described as a fictional "making of" feature about *Citizenfour*, Laura Poitras's Oscar-winning documentary on the former National Security Agency contractor Edward J. Snowden (Tallerico, 2016).

With early stages of globalisation and the convergence of a shared global identity, what was previously a monologue had transformed into a dialogue – a form of communication where sensory input and information flow and reception worked both ways.

In our present day post-dialogue world, millions of conversations and exchanges erupt around the world in an iota of a second. The information we relay across the web – including our innermost desires and feelings is binary and therefore, can be accessed, making individual identity a thin smoke screen.

This analysis of the movie *Snowden*, which was released in 2016, and is inspired by real life events plots the concept of personal identity in relation to questions of liberty, privacy, security and power.

Snowden as a movie deploys the technique of flashbacks for its runtime of 2 hours and 14 minutes. This aids the audience in analysing the character in his entirety. The exposure into Snowden's past equips one with adequate socio-political and historical background to relate the coordinates of the movie with the temporal realities of the time. The structure of the movie skilfully explores the fissures in personal, professional and national identity of the protagonist. The opening scene places one directly at the center of all the tension, inside Snowden's hotel room at The Mira in Hong Kong where he sits down with journalists, exposing the biggest nexus of government lies and propaganda in contemporary history. In terms of semiotics, it is significant to notice the aura of secrecy maintained throughout the movie. Strips covering webcams, mobile phones kept in the microwave and Snowden's aversion to cameras are some examples. The use of the rubik's cube as an important symbol is central to understanding Snowden's story. The movie, based on true events, explores the protagonist's inner conflicts, which he is constantly confronted with.

The movie succeeds in rousing strong nationalist sentiments in the audience right from the opening scenes. In a glimpse of Snowden's past, we are taken to his military training days for the Special Forces, one hears the troops singing "Went from driving Cadillacs, to driving convoys in Iraq" in unison, thus invoking images of American patriotism. Furthermore, Snowden's senior at the training asks him to "rip (his) heart out" to be able to serve the country. The significance of this scene is that it provides the audience vantage points to traverse through the narrative. National Identity as a concept is associated strongly with militarism and safeguarding National Interests (Klobuszewska, 2018). After breaking his leg, Snowden is shown at a Central Intelligence Agency (CIA) recruitment interview where he meets Senior Instructor Corbin O'Brian.

Corbin O'Brian:"You wanted to be special forces."
Edward Snowden: Yes, sir"
Corbin O'Brian:"Why do you want to join the CIA?"
Edward Snowden:"I'd like to help my country make a difference in the world."

Snowden's guiding ethos is that he wants to be of use to his nation. One question of symbolic importance remains 'Do you believe the USA is the greatest country in the world?' on the polygraph. This question largely defines the ethical dilemmas of the character. He starts out with a definitive yes to the question but as the narrative unfolds, he turns more and more sceptical due to the ugly truths about the nature of his work that lie exposed.

During the training period, Brian asserts "Bombs will not stop terrorism, brains will" which plots the story in relation to questions of soft power and the role of the US government in maintaining global hegemony in world of the web.

For a major part of the film, Snowden's personal life has been covered with great finesse. His relationship with photographer Lindsay Mills makes him question his Manichean view of his commitment to national interests and the government. Right after they meet, they cross a site of protest with citizens holding posters that read 'Drop Bush Not Bombs!' responding to the aftermath of 9/11 and the regime's War on Terror. While Lindsay signs the petition to stop bombing, Edward lets it pass. "I just don't really like bashing my country" is what he tells her, after which she says, "It is my country too and right now, it has blood on its hands."

Snowden's moment of truth arrives when he is sent on a mission to Geneva, Switzerland in 2007. He gains access to XKEYSCORE and PRISM, software which enable him to spy on anybody, anywhere in the world without obtaining a legitimate Foreign Intelligence Surveillance Act (FISA) Court order as he had been instructed during his CIA training. He quickly learns the tricks and loopholes of his trade and realises that top government officials are at complete liberty to flout the laws in the name of 'national security'. To confront any questions of personal identity in the 21st century one must keenly look at the epistemological fractures in our understanding of privacy and how the flow of information has still not been decolonised. Cases of non-consensual pornography showing up on the internet brings to the forefront the horrific realisation of being under a watchful radar, every second that we live. From what's on our tables to what goes on inside our bedrooms, the schism between the public and the private has been violently amalgamated, which is a shocking discovery for Snowden.

Since power dynamics across the world have undergone immense change since the birth of a New World Order, our conception of power has also considerably shift from a purely material, militaristic understanding and show of strength to Soft Power which introduces concepts like a complete reification and liquidation of an individual into a binary digit or a piece of data. With databases of these irreducible details, global hegemons can technologically create a proscenium of everything - from influencing and manipulating our desires to selling us things we do not need to influence our ideologies, and access to pedagogy based on the behavioural choices we inhibit every time we enter the world of binary digits. The movie talks about the existence of US networks in Japan and friendly countries like Belgium, Brazil, Germany - which do not pose a direct threat to US interests. This is when he realises that "Terrorism is the excuse. This is about economic and social control. And the only thing you're really protecting is the supremacy of your government."

Snowden quickly grasps the meta scale of data mining when he is supposed to find links to 'dirty Saudi money'. He befriends a Pakistani banker and spies on his connections to find out that his daughter is dating an illegal immigrant, who is soon deported. What ensues is life risking for the girl, and the nonchalance with which Snowden's senior addresses this makes him question the nature of his work.

Snowden:"And if his daughter had died?"

Undercover CIA Agent:"We could've used that too."

Snowden:"Are you serious? What, in the name of a promotion?"

There are snippets of Obama's campaign scattered across the movie. Snowden believes with a change of government, things might get better; however he admits he was wrong. A key scene to understanding Snowden's breakdown is when he makes love to Lindsay. During his most intimate moments, he cannot help but think about himself as a subject of surveillance as well. He watches his webcam with horror. Furthermore, when he has an argument with Lindsay in Japan, the screenplay zooms out creating the effect of a "recording". The message of the movie becomes clear then - no matter who you are, you are being watched. This further problematises his relationship, as he is bound by non-disclosure agreements with the government and cannot explain his internal dilemmas to Lindsay.

There is a brief point in the movie where Snowden quits his job and moves to Maryland to lead a 'happy' life with his girlfriend. His belief that he'd be able to start anew is soon shattered when he hears about three NSA agents who had their homes raided by the Federal Bureau of Investigation simply because they had filed legal complaints for abuse of powers and overreach by the officials working in cybersecurity for the United States government. The words "Do not tell truth to power, we'll hammer you" echo deep inside his head, which makes him realise that the State machinery cannot be defeated or exposed easily.

The movie accurately establishes connect and sequence between the chronology of the scenes. Right after this he meets Brian who tells him "Most Americans do not want Freedom. They want security." which prompts Snowden to think that ordinary people did not make that choice for themselves and are not aware of the being under the radar of a global spying machine. As he questions the idea of freedom of choice, basic civil liberties and rights being compromised, Brian, who comes across as a malicious and shrewd government official, offers him a post in Hawaii which he says, would enable Snowden to get 'on top of his career'. Unable to decide what to choose between duty and ethics, Snowden's disenfranchisement becomes visible when he suffers a paralytic attack. However, he still moves to Hawaii with Lindsay.

The relationship between Lindsay and Edward is the key to the film, since it establishes what is at stake for the hero as he faces the conflicting demands of love and duty. It also affirms that he is a nice, normal, humble guy, neither a zealot nor an egomaniac. (Scott, 2016).

What leads to the climax of the movie is Lindsay's birthday. Snowden's colleagues from the CIA talk about US air strikes where children were targeted and how watching visuals where "they are gone in a cloud of dust" are a part of the job and have become routine so much so that the colleagues laugh while recounting these encounters. Snowden discusses the criminal nature of jobs and how ordinary people following orders sometimes have wider social ramifications. He mentions the Nazi regime, wherein normal people went about carrying legal orders, which resulted in the Holocaust. The Nuremberg Trials find mention in this conversation where these 'normal people' were tried. By the time we reach this scene, the audience can affirm that Snowden's beliefs that the system is unjust have concretised. This is a teeth-gritting moment, as the audience will finally know how he managed to 'steal' such vast amounts of classified data from one of the most heavily protected sites in the world. He suffers another paralytic attack here and is now set to do the right thing to lay his internal chaos to an end.

"The kid did it!" is what Forrester, Snowden's teacher at the CIA training exclaims when his 'data leaks' are made public, leading to a public uproar. The scene at the end echoes the complete opposite sentiment of Snowden's stance on questioning the government at the beginning.

After he is done filming the documentary, he passes on the Rubik's cube to Laura, the journalist responsible for fair reporting of his story. This scene is symbolic as it shows that the conflict at the heart of the protagonist has finally been solved. Even though the US government charges him with theft and espionage, he regains a sense of identity once he fulfils his moral duty. Staying true to his ethical obligations, he deletes all the data he has from his drive after passing it on to senior journalists from The Guardian.

The US government is rattled, and the movie shows Obama addressing Snowden as a 'hacker' and constantly justifying the use of spyware by the government. However, the truth is out in plain sight and due to mass protests and worldwide media coverage, Snowden escapes.

"We will not be silenced. I lost a stable life but gained a new one," is his final message as an asylum seeker in Moscow, 'live from the internet' on a talk show.

The ending credits of the movie spin around montages of news clippings that detail the aftermath of the Snowden leaks, the Obama administration regulating data mining and real life candids of Snowden and Lindsay. One is confronted with the fact that people who take up strong moral positions and tell truth to power are ordinary people, just like us, who withstand extraordinary risks and put their lives on the line for the greater good. Snowden is not just a movie, it is a cinematic experience that defines the heroes of our age.

In conclusion the movie leaves the onlooker with a realisation that complete technological neurosis defines the character of our age, with our lives and their most perfunctory details available on a screen. The paramount question to pose here is: how do we ensure what's private remains private? From the ambit of the workplace to the bathroom, technology has made modern lives easier but has also strategically placed us under a panopticon (Foucault, 1977). We're constantly being watched, analysed and recorded, which causes a subsequent breakdown in personal identity.

Time and again there have been whistle blowers and potent research that have shown that users are indeed concerned about their privacy within the Social Web, but do not apply these concerns to their usage behaviour. This is known as the 'privacy paradox' (Barnes, 2006). Therefore, to understand the cracks in personal identity, we as active agents need to confront this paradox.

References

Snowden (2016). [DVD] Directed by O. Stone. Hollywood.

Tallerico, B. (2016). *Snowden Movie Review & Film Summary (2016) | Roger Ebert*. [online] Rogerebert.com. Available at: https://www.rogerebert.com/reviews/snowden-2016 [Accessed 27 Apr. 2018].

Scott, A. (2016). *Review: 'Snowden,' Oliver Stone's Restrained Portrait of a Whistle-Blower*. [online] Nytimes.com. Available at: https://www.nytimes.com/2016/09/16/movies/snowden-review-oliver-stone-joseph-gordon-levitt.html [Accessed 27 Apr. 2018].

Klobuszewska, U. (2018). *The Creation of a National Identity through Militarization – Urban Labs*. [online] Urbanlabsce.eu. Available at: http://urbanlabsce.eu/982-2/ [Accessed 1 May 2018].

Foucault, M. (1977). *Discipline and punish*. New York: Pantheon Books.

Barnes, S. (2006). *A privacy paradox: Social networking in the United States*. [online] Journals.uic.edu. Available at: http://journals.uic.edu/ojs/index.php/fm/article/view/1394/1312 [Accessed 1 May 2018].

Fryed Pears - *Arcadia* by Iain Pears reviewed by L. Shapley Bassen

Over the December 2015 holidays, I missed my chance to see J.J.Abrams's new STAR WARS THE FORCE AWAKENS in 3-D and didn't see the point of going to a 2-D showing.

Marshall McLuhan's 1964 dictum, "The medium is the message," has never been more zeitgeist true than now. Three years ago in autumn, it turns out, J.J. Abrams collaborated with author Doug Dorst on a much-heralded hardback novel titled just *S*. "The multilayered conceit of the thing almost makes it a play interacting with a book. That is, there is the novel itself (*Ship of Theseus*), which stands alone as its own story, and then there are the notes in the margins: a conversation and investigation and mystery and love story between two people, which is both connected to and separate from the central text. Then, there is the editor of the book, who appears in an introduction and in footnotes. So there were many characters and points of view to balance. It felt less like film or TV, and more like concocting something insane and very special."
http://www.nytimes.com/2013/10/27/books/review/j-j-abrams-by-the-book.html

That same May, 2013, author Iain Pears was invited to give a seminar talk at Oxford, which he called *Egos in Arcadia: Telling tales in a digital age.* The clever pun of the title of his book/iPad app then work-in-progress alluded to the 17th century Poussin paintings of a tomb in a pastoral idyll and echoed the classical phrase, *Et in Arcadia ego*, whose translation ["Even in Arcadia, there am I"] is a reminder of 4th dimensional, temporal perspective: in the midst of even the best of Life, Death is present.

And now for a 21st century, more than 3-D version/vision of *Arcadia* by novelist Iain Pears that takes the Abrams/Dorst recipe up an Emeril Lagasse notch, BAM! Gluten-free and delicious utopia/dystopia, Time, and Story are major ingredients in *Arcadia*. No need to rue the roux: mixtures of metaphor and everything else stirred together in *Arcadia* make it a truly movable feast. Also no need for me to repeat the rave review summaries that the novel began to receive last autumn; they do a fine job of guiding you through the book's mobius strip structure that also calls to mind Escher's famous portrait of *Relativity*. The hearty takeaway/takeout I'd like to share is that anyone interested in cooking up a story would be well-served by sous-chef Pears, whose new novel *Arcadia*, together with Chef Northrop Frye's *Anatomy of Criticism*, would make a *cordon bleu* semester course in any MFA writing program. Bon appétit!
Arcadia is Faber & Faber's first novel to have been written primarily with digital readers in mind. The British publishers believe it to be the first book of its kind in existence. Shortly after its iPad appearance http://www.telegraph.co.uk/books/what-to-read/faber-iain-pearsarcadia-app/, the 596 page hardback was published last September 3rd.

This February, 2016, Knopf presents a 528 page US edition. "While the hardback is 180,000 words, the app comes to 250,000, offering additional stories and expanding those told in the hardback." In all iterations, its main character is a British contemporary of [Canadian] Marshall McLuhan named Henry Lytten, a 50-something Oxford don in 1960, who is also a fantasy writer [in an Inklings-like afterhours group] and a retired WWII spy. Henry Lytten meets his incarnation, Henary the Storyteller, in a 26th century post-apocalyptic, pastoral England that is the result of the novel's sci fi time machine plot. Henry and Henary cross paths in an Arcadian Arden-forest complete with not just one Rosalind [Rosie], but two.

This interview with Iain Pears http://bryanappleyard.com/iain-pears-arcadia-by-a-chap/ sums up nicely: "The three plot lines in the book are: a realist spy fiction set in the 1960s; a sci-fi one set centuries later in a nightmarish overpopulated world; and a fantasy one in a rural paradise, Anterwold… Woven in with this are landscapes derived from Claude Lorrain, a curious girl rather like Lewis Carroll's Alice, scenes from *AS YOU LIKE IT*, and asides on and references to Tolkien and C.S. Lewis. But, unlike both those authors, Pears rigorously excludes magic. 'The fantasy bit is without gods or magic. Tolkien almost did that, but he always slips in a bit of magic, and C.S.Lewis depends on magic. But I didn't want any talking lions. The point about Anterwold is that it's an attempt to create an ideal, stable society that could actually exist.' It's all fantastic fun and, in spite of its complexity, a swift read. It is divided into chunks made deliberately bite-sized, in deference to the reading habits of the young, but which also spare the tired minds of the old… Pears got his crucial idea from an article he read in a science magazine, which said that many of the problems of physics would be solved if time could be disregarded and everything happened simultaneously — a notion used in the movie *Interstellar*." From The Independent, http://www.independent.co.uk/arts-entertainment/books/reviews/arcadia-by-iain-pears-book-review-a-near-perfect-take-on-the-perils-of-a-paralleluniverse-a6672251.html, readers are wisely advised to "treat this novel, and its app, as a memepark where a whole menagerie of tropes, themes, myths and motifs from centuries of fantasy and romance can frolic
"As Rosie remarks about Anterwold, 'You steal ideas from everyone.' Shakespeare, Sidney, Carroll, Bradbury, Huxley, Orwell, Tolkien-and-Lewis, Le Carré, Fleming – to label *Arcadia* as 'derivative' would be both to miss and to make Pears's point. In a world (or worlds) menaced by terminal risks, he builds a story-ark: a granary or seedbank of genres."

When you read the novel in hardback, the stop-start intercutting of chapters becomes an experience of time travel in/of itself. 19th century Dickens and 20th century Azimov are more consistently linear, but 21st century Pears intentionally leaps from locales/characters to others so that your first experience of every chapter is getting your bearings again, literally finding yourself at the same time as you do the characters/story lines. The hardback reading results in a real suspension of routine experience of linear time reality. The digital rendering of the whiskedtogether stories allows a reader to follow the addition of one ingredient at a time, but that freedom implies that 2D is an illusion. *At the same time* contrasts with *one at a time* to great cumulative effect: [1] recognition of the questionable reality of our primate-evolved, cause/effect linear assumptions about Time; [2] recognition that *Arcadia* moves *free of time* just as subatomic particles do and *we can in memory and speculation*. This is real fun and food for thought.
And now, to the Fry[e]ing pan: Iain Pears plays a game of friendly three card monte not only with spacetime, but also with storytelling formats. One of the most influential literary critics of the 20th century, Northrop Frye, would frolic through Pears's pages/screen. Frye's four *Anatomy* modes are the destinies manifest in *Arcadia*.
Just follow the seasons. Spring: Mistaken identities and disguises revealed at story's end come right out of Comedy mode, as does the Angela-mother/Emily-daughter generational hand off. Comedy is the vernal promise of reconciliation of the old generation with the new, and it usually ends with a celebration/ wedding/party. Summer: The Asimov-worthy sci-fi plot [consider the time travel novel

The End of Eternity and short story *Spell My Name with an* S] pits a dystopian evil villain Oldmanter [name out of Dickens] against a dynamic duo of time machine maker mother and her daughter, an environmental/cultural conservator reminiscent of *Fahrenheit 451*. When superhuman good defeats superhuman evil, you're reading/writing Romance. *Autumn: Tragedy* is the story of homicidal disorder caused by flawed superiority with order restored at great but ennobling cost. In *Arcadia*, time travel enfolds the tragedy of atomic apocalypse within its overriding Romance plot. Winter: When dystopia prevails or utter confusion of definitions of identity/reality takes over [also momentarily in Star Trek Next Generation's Moriarty holodeck episode, "Ship in a Bottle"], you're in Irony. But since Pears serves up the wish fulfillment half of Frye's wheel [Comedy/Romance] rather than the realistic quandrants [Tragedy/Irony], freedom relieves entrapment in most, but not all, cases.

MFA Alert: Frye's catalogs in *The Anatomy of Criticism* mean that readers, students, and writers of stories need not reinvent the wheel, but just keep the one above snowballing into the future just as Pears does in *Arcadia*. There, nothing is ever lost but stays afloat in his "story-ark" when a time-traveling scholar-author meets a facet of himself in a future society where Storytellers are its most valued citizens. Consider the creative power of *recognizing* pattern: you need not get lost in history, nor repeat it. Instead, it can be a guide to your own story.

Together, Frye's *Anatomy* and Pears's *Arcadia* are a buoyant ark of literary covenant, encyclopedia and study guide for a superior full semester course. Some savvy 21st century students could even create their own digital iPad concordium of the critical primer and novel. Either way, hardback or digital, reading *Arcadia* is as mind-altering as walking on a mobius strip. *Star Wars* J.J. Abrams's 2-dimensional novel S. has much in common with Pears's *Arcadia*, the real digital 3-D deal that calls for film adaptation. It even ends with the promise of a sequel. May the Force be with it.

Jane Simmons reviews Carolyn Jess-Cooke: *Boom!*

ISBN-13: 9781781721759

Published by Seren

Carolyn Jess-Cooke

Carolyn Jess-Cooke was born in Belfast, Northern Ireland in 1978 and currently lives in north-east England. She is mother to four children. Her debut poetry collection *Inroads* (Seren, 2010) received a Northern Promise Award, an Eric Gregory Award, the Tyrone Guthrie Prize for Poetry, and was shortlisted for the New London Poetry Prize. Her debut novel *The Guardian Angel's Journal* (Little, Brown/Piatkus, 2011) was published in 23 languages and her second novel, *The Boy Who Could See Demons* (Piatkus, 2012) was critically appraised by *The New York Times, The Guardian, Booklist,* and others. A number of her poetry commissions are featured in public art installations around England, including a poem set into a 700m ribbon of steel that runs throughout a mental health complex in Middlesbrough. She has performed her work at many festivals and venues around the world, including the Sydney Writers' Festival, the Irish Writers Centre and at the Sage Gateshead.

The title poem of this collection, *Boom!* describes the moment when the new baby arrives in the poet's family *like a hand grenade.*

This baby *who thought she was a hand-grenade* explodes into their lives with such violence that she throws them from their *orbit.* The language and imagery of war continue throughout the poem. This explosive device of a baby emits *endless alarm-sounds* which are *difficult to decode* – it is a situation which will be immediately recognised by any parents. Then *more such devices entered our lives* and the parents face the prospect that *each day may be our last* in fact, they are blown *to smithereens* but they *held on* and

shrapnel soldered the parts of us

that hadn't quite fit before

The poems then look back to the early weeks of the poet's first pregnancy, and describe an early scan in the poem *Anonymous* before moving on to the final weeks leading up to *Home Birth.* The poet describes the birth, using domestic language and imagery appropriate to the domestic surroundings where the birth takes place.

They said she was stuck

As though she was a nine pound human fork

Pronged in the dishwasher

before moving into a contrasting description of the birth of her second baby, a son

my body remembered,

it took the first shunt of his head, yawned, then

toboganned him out in a rush of brine,

red as a crab

The poems capture the rapturous moments of parenthood, such as when the mother observes her baby in the poem *The Waking*. The details of the description are minute, full of emotion, and often tactile,

Those first few days every part of her wakened,

the seedling eyes stirred by sunlight, tight fists

clamped to her chest like a medieval knight

and slowly loosening as if the metal hands

were reminded of their likeness to petals

by the flowing hours. Her colours, too,

rose up like disturbed oils in a lake, pooling

through the birth-tinge into human shades,

her ink eyes lightening to an ancestral blue,

the scurf and residue of me on her scalp floated

easily as a pollen from the sweet grass of her hair.

She reminded me of a fern, each morning more

unfurled, the frond-limbs edging away from her

heart, the wide leaves of her face spread to catch

my gaze. Once, I saw the white down of her skin

cloud in my hands, the cream ridges of her nails

drift like crescent moons, the thick blue rope

she had used to descend me tossed like a stone,

as though she was finally free.

Seen through the eyes of her children, the world is a remarkably beautiful and wonderful place – marvels are discovered in the most unexpected places and in the simplest of things – and the poet also describes these experiences with an intense appreciation. At times, it seems as though the fresh eyes and new vision of her children are shaping or extending her abilities or powers as a poet *flooding the world* for her. There is

a kind of purpose

only she defines. Because of her, the simple is no more

and

my darling's breath determines there

to be nothing but hope, and life, and plenty.

114

These changes are perhaps best summed up in the phrase *all life re-quickened.*

To counter-balance the moments of ecstasy or rapture, there are also tragi-comic sleepless nights, full of *small elbows in the face* and *assailed by colds and colic.* Neither does the poet shy away from the darker fears and depressions that can afflict the parents of babies and young children.

In the early weeks or months of her baby's life, the poet seems to believe that the infant is some sort of changeling or foundling, not hers at all, and she is afraid that

the right ones will come and claim this

foreign jewel someone entrusted to you

In *The Lotteries*, she counts the many ways in which she and her baby have both been lucky to survive – they return home *under the gold light of luck* and benefit from *a cornucopia of blessings -* whereas, elsewhere in the world, others are not so lucky

somewhere out there some other child has not woken.

Later in the collection, she is afraid when she is unable to find her child on a crowded beach – an experience she describes in the poem *What Matters.*

The poet is affected by post-natal depression – an experience which she describes in the two poems, *The Sadness* and *Parallelism.* In both poems, she uses the form to represent how the experience manifests itself. In *Sadness*, the lines are irregular in length, and the whole poem is off-centre, veering away – line by line – from the left-hand margin of the page, each line beginning that little bit further in. It makes reading the poem an unsettling experience in itself, even before the language and imagery begin their work of evoking a sense of the pervading sadness which afflicts the poet and which cannot be shaken off. In *Parallelism*, the poet again uses the form of the poem to good effect. It is written in couplets, the first of which states

I hid from Depression

  It found me

Once more, the layout has an unsettling effect which accumulates as, in each couplet, she describes how she tries to escape and how every time *Depression* finds her. The personification of depression, its capitalisation, and its repetition throughout the poem, all contribute to the sense of an all pervasive and inescapable state of mind. Even when the depression lifts at the end of the poem, the poet knows that she has not really escaped

When Depression left, a note read

I will be back

and the lack of a full-stop at the end of the line makes the threat all the more convincing. The conflicting sides of motherhood are later explored further in the poem *Motherhood Diptych,* where the poet once again uses the form of the poem on the page to enhance the presentation of the ideas explored.

The earlier poems in the collection explore the poet's personal experience of motherhood – often dealing with experiences and emotions which will be familiar to the readers. However, as the collection builds, the poems begin to show that the experience of parenthood is not just personal – it is public and it is political. This can be seen in the poems *The Only Dad at Playgroup*, *Working Mother*, *Staying at Home*, or *Poem Made from Bits of Newspaper Headlines*.

Readers who are interested in exploring more of this poet's work might also like to know about the *Writing Motherhood* project. Carolyn Jess-Cooke founded this project which has since resulted in the publication of her recent anthology of poems *Writing Motherhood* (Seren, 2017).

Over Land, Over Sea: poems for those seeking refuge – by co-editor of the book, Emma Lee

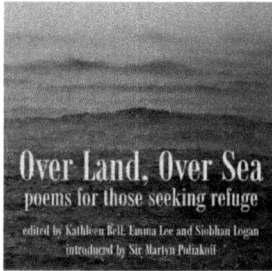

The idea for *Over Land, Over Sea: poems for those seeking refuge* (Five Leaves, 2015) started in August 2015 with a Facebook group bringing together the publisher, co-editors and supporters before a call for submissions was issued on 2 September 2015. It rose from the need to give voice to the alarm that was shared among poets at the suffering and hardship people who are seeking refuge were and still are experiencing. Some contributors expressed relief at being given an opportunity to provide a counter-narrative to the one offered by the media and by being able to write and talk about how they felt about what was happening and a chance to show solidarity with people seeking refuge.

The anthology enabled poets to become active: it made connections and empowered poets to write, speak and raise funds to help others. Some had been vicariously traumatised and dealt with that trauma by writing about what they were seeing and what they felt about what they had witnessed and were still witnessing. Many of those responding did so by writing poems because poetry is turned to at times of extreme emotion. People in "The Jungle" had witnessed war, suffered bereavement, injuries and trauma. They were living from one moment to the next, still hoping and dreaming of reaching a place of safety or to be reunited with family. Poetry's brevity, structure and texture gives it a perfect framework in which to explore feelings and experiences the writer is struggling to articulate, which would sprawl, expand, loosen and deviate without bringing clarity in prose. Poetry pushes writers to strip ideas down, to focus on what they are saying and how they are saying it. It is as much about the space around the poem's words as it is about the words. Poetic devices such as metaphors or analogies offer a way of exploring and expressing a subject without being explicit. Both traditional forms and free verse offer a way of bringing some order to disorganised, disorientated thinking.

On 1 December 2015 *Over Land, Over Sea: poems for those seeking refuge* was published to raise funds for Medecins Sans Frontieres, Leicester City of Sanctuary and Nottingham Refugee Forum and has raised over £3000. In total 204 poems were received from Europe, Iraq, Australia and America. Due to practicalities and time pressures the anthology only included poems in English, a language common to all three co-editors. Despite the anthology being monolingual, the support was still tremendous.

There were similar initiatives such as Eyewear's *refugees welcome*, which included 24 poems from 24 poets, was published later in December 2015, Marie Lightman's *Writers for Calais Refugees* blog, which sought to raise awareness of refugees' plight was set up on 30 August 2015 and throughout 2016 there were various Poem-A-Thons, where poets were sponsored to read poems to raise funds.

To begin with *Over Land, Over Sea: poems for those seeking refuge* was a print publication. Subsequently readings were held in Leicester; Nottingham; at the StAnza Poetry Festival at St Andrews in Scotland and at the Poetry Cafe in London and some of those readings were at the invitation of Leicester's Human Rights Arts and Film Festival, the Leicester Migration Network at

117

Leicester University and London-based Exiled Writers Ink. The readings, and Facebook group, offered contributors the chance to meet each other and build a sense of community. By making connections with poetry readers and other poets, we were building awareness that poets weren't powerless, they could do something. They can write. They can give readings. They have a voice. They can talk about why they are writing and giving the readings. They can lend their voice to a cause. And they can raise funds for people who are seeking refuge.

Since publication, there has been a Journeys Poems Pop-up Library where postcards featuring poems from the anthology were handed out to travellers at Leicester Railway Station. Travelling is an ideal time to read or think about other journeys and reading is about sharing stories and making journeys in the imagination. The postcards, featuring eight of the poems from *Over Land, Over Sea: poems for those seeking refuge* were given out to encourage people to think about current and historical journeys undertaken by people seeking refuge and to inspire and encourage conversation. Two contributors to *Over Land, Over Sea: poems for those seeking refuge* read poems at the Day of Sanctuary at the Houses of Parliament in London on 29 November 2016.

With *Over Land, Over Sea: poems for those seeking refuge* it was acknowledged that a disadvantage of the original anthology was that it was monolingual. *Journeys in Translation*, which builds on the success of the Journeys Poems Pop-up Library, therefore encourages poets and translators to translate the poems into other languages and organise readings of the original English poems alongside translations with discussions around the difficulties in translating poems either from English or into English. *Journeys in Translation* is not restricted to fluent bi- or multi-lingual poets and translators but includes people who are learning a language or have some language skills they are not confident in so that they can develop those skills and gain confidence. For example one participant has translated some of the poems into her mother tongue, Arabic, and now feels more confident using English. One *Journeys in Translation* session, run in conjunction with a refugee charity, encouraged those who were learning English to pick phrases from the poems they recognised and translate them into another language. The project has also provoked discussions around cultural translations. For example one poem uses space as a metaphor for the alienation and othering of refugees. This caused difficulties for one poet attempting to translate the poem into Shona because there was no direct translation for some of the astronomical terms.

Emma Lee

Over Land, Over Sea: poems for those seeking refuge is available from Five Leaves: https://fiveleavesbookshop.co.uk/over-land-over-sea/

The Journeys in Translation blog is at http://journeysintranslation.wordpress.com

New Essays

Every so often I receive an email from a website called Chessworld.net. It says, 'Nigel, we've missed you at Chessworld.' They certainly have. I've gone missing. They've lost me.

I like to think that the people – real human beings – running the site have relegated me to a folder of chess players who have similarly gone AWOL, but who might be tempted to switch to a 'live' folder and take up the game again, like returning prodigals.

I never respond but I do wonder about Tafadzwa, a player from Malawi with whom I was paired for my first game on the worldwide web. That's what Chessworld.net is: a means of playing the game remotely. I think you used to be able to do it by phone, but that took ages. Chess on the internet is instantaneous, which is probably what made me leave Tafadzwa floating in a swarm of megabytes: work – as a writer – and other commitments meant I might take days over one move, whereas Tafadzwa, clearly transfixed by the computer screen and probably a grandmaster-in-waiting, responded within hours, possibly minutes or seconds.

Since the emails expressing regret at my absence never mention Tafadzwa, I assume he (she) regarded me as a lost cause and has now been linked with some other opponent, perhaps on the outskirts of Helsinki ('Hello, Tapio, your next game is with Tafadzwa, from Liwande, in Malawi.') I think I was on my sixth move, an early and back-pedalling Knight to Queen's Rook 3, when I left Tafadzwa virtually dangling from the edge of the virtual chess board. .

I'm no doubt politically incorrect in visualising her (him) as a brightly-dressed five-year-old prodigy, surrounded by other brightly-dressed prodigies, sitting in the corrugated tin shack that serves as their village school and community centre, where their teacher, wearing a white shirt and tie despite the heat and with sweat patches under his arm the shape of the Democratic Republic of the Congo, is nominally in charge of the second-hand computer he acquired for them three months before. I've clearly forgotten to be PC when writing about playing chess on a PC.

Probably still with only a dial-up connection to the internet, Tafadzwa nonetheless managed to respond to my moves thirty times faster than I made them. And if it's impossible to get a radio, let alone a computer, to work in a Malawian outpost so described without attaching it via a belt to a fixed bicycle pedalled to a searing wattage by the teacher and his colleagues, my excuse for imagining the scene thus is that Tafadzwas everywhere deserve to have a computer with superfast broadband so that they can put it about me in my leisurely European domicile and take me down a peg or three.

The point about those emails is that only when I receive them do I remember that I'd forgotten about them. At least I know what they're getting at: my tardiness. I suppose I'll keep receiving them after I'm dead. I wish I could apologise to Tafadzwa for leaving him (her) suspended. Then again, perhaps she (he) is Professor Tafadzwa Makalamba of the Mzuzu Bible College; not an eight-year-old chess prodigy at all but an academic simply wishing to improve his (her) game while taking time off from translating the Biblia Sacra Vulgata into the Nyakyusa-Ngonde dialect. These speculations are yet another way of keeping my brain working. Renewing an acquaintance with chess was another, As I had spent many years failing to see more than three moves ahead, I thought that if I could increase that to four or even five my brain had yet to fulfil its potential at a time when it was supposed to be running down at the rate of a million dead brain cells per hour. My old school pal Godfrey Brangham is a serious chess player, who can do what the Fischers and Kasparovs can do without blinking and remember a whole game, his moves and his opponent's, from start to finish. I can recite to myself Yeats's *Sailing To Byzantium* after learning it a year ago and refreshing my memory every few weeks, usually in bed and on the borders of sleep. Ditto several other poems, including the awkward *Binsey Poplars* by Gerard Manley Hopkins ('When we, even when we mean/to mend her we end her').

I started keeping a 'remembrance notebook' years ago. I was never much good at it, often forgetting that I'd promised myself to make an entry every few days. It began as a working title for things I wanted to set down as a hedge against the possibility or likelihood of forgetting: the immediate present becoming the retrievable past. The word 'remembrance' also has connotations of self-aggrandisement, the idea that one should be remembered, like the war dead.

One thing I'll never forget is that I never went to war, though my country's infantry seems always to have been tramping across some foreign terrain or other in my name during my lifetime. An anti-war friend of mine once confessed that he'd never offer a lift to a hitch-hiking soldier. I sympathised but I'm not a pacifist; that's to say, I've never bother to give pacifism or my attraction to it a thought. Another friend, provocative to a fault, thought that registering as a conscientious objector was more brave than running full tilt at a machine-gun post. I can still remember all these controversial views.

My grandfathers, I recall, never went to war, because they were coalminers. Time was when I could locate my paternal grandfather's virtually unmarked grave (at least there was no gravestone, just a metal marker with a number on it); now I neither visit it nor wonder if it is still traceable in the long grass. Out of sight, out of mind.

Keeping my brain working is imperative at my age, which is why I started a blog (www.NigelJarrett.wordpress.com) so that (a) everything I can currently remember is recorded; and (b) when I can't even recall the permanently remembered, someone else might let me know what I made of what I could still, against the mass immolation of my brain cells, bring immediately to mind.

Is this important? It's important.

The past is what we have, secure if ever open to interpretation and significance. The present is always uncertain, though often and mostly gratifying. The future is wholly unknowable, yet a vacuum awaiting infinite possibility.

The past, too, is the almost instantaneous transformation of the present, minute by minute, second by second. Nothing lasts in the present; it's continuously filing into the background, into storage – if we're lucky. Into the past we pour our present joys and travails. I can see that some would wish to forget the past, or diminish its importance.

We used to live near Mady Gerrard, who had survived Auschwitz as a young girl and took part in the forced march to Bergen-Belsen, where she was liberated by the British. She eventually fetched up in New York, Her childhood skill as a knitter in Hungary served her well, because she became one of America's leading knitwear designers, making clothes for Mrs Pat Nixon, Dionne Warwick, Shirley Hampshire and others, including an ancient silent movie star, Celeste Holm, who flew to New York from her home in Florida, or LA, to be measured and fitted out.

I wrote a story about that, called *El Cid*, the title a reference to another episode of mis-remembering, the (fictional) Celeste arriving in Manhattan, meeting my fictionalised former neighbour, now a film buff, and claiming to have been in line for a leading part in an earlier, pre-talkie version of the film that's also the title of my story. She'd forgotten, had Celeste, and had also claimed to have been considered for a part in a film directed by D. W. Griffith.

Anyway, Mady wrote an autobiography, in which her experience in the concentration camps constituted barely one-third of her memoir. When readers queried this, she said her life was about survival and that had lasted longer than her incarceration, and needed to be celebrated at far greater length. Just over sixty years after she was freed from Belsen she met the British officer who had been on hand to open the gates. She saw his picture in the Daily Telegraph, illustrating a piece about Holocaust Day, and as it was of him as a young officer, she recognised it and got in touch. He didn't know her, but she remembered him.

The internet enables us to lose people we never met. It's a digital loss in cyberspace. I have lost chess-playing Tafadzwa as completely as she (he) has lost me. I might even get an *El Cid* story out of that. Writing is a means of not forgetting, even though, like Iris Murdoch, one might eventually forget that one ever wrote anything. One might even forget that one used to remember, not knowing what remembering is – or, for that matter, forgetting.

A Black California Baby-Boomer by Aurora M. Lewis

I don't know exactly when it came to me, maybe in 1960 when I was ten. I saw Ruby Bridges on television walking with White men dressed in suits, escorting her down those stone building steps on her first day at school. Perhaps it was when I heard someone shout nigger at her? Just when did I become aware that there may be people who hated me as well? Ruby was so small, surrounded by screaming White people, their faces contorted with hatred, Ruby's little face so frightened. I was afraid for her and for myself because I could be her. The image of Ruby resonated with me throughout my childhood, such contempt for a little Black girl who just wanted to go to school.

I was born in 1950, Los Angeles California. We lived in Avalon Gardens, a diverse low- income public housing project. Originally, it was built for veterans, with green lawns, oleander bushes, and purple jacaranda trees. My father had been a hospital orderly when he returned from the Korean War, but in 1957 he became an L.A. County Sheriff, the first of five Blacks to join the force. With the raise in income, he purchased a house in Compton, California using his VA. Benefits. Back then Compton was predominately White. However, a housing development was built specifically for Black Vets. I remember that my parents were so excited because there was no down payment required and we would be moving from the projects.

As mentioned, my father served in the Korean War, as had my uncle, who also purchased a home in the same housing development. Most of the children at my school were White. There were other Black children in my class, about four or five, and we pretty much stuck together. They all lived in that same housing development. Our teacher was nice but, seemed to look through us most of the time, seldom calling on us. I have a sensing that she just tolerated us. We all sat together in the back of the classroom.

One of our class activities was role play with several large doll houses and farms. In both cases a boy and girl played the roles of the mother and father. Another boy and girl played the son and daughter. This day, we were going to do role play with the doll houses. It was my turn, I was hopeful that a Black boy named Gerard would be my pretend husband. He had curly brown hair and light brown eyes, I thought he was cute. Instead the teacher selected another boy, Joe Louis (named after the boxer) because our last names sounded the same. I was so disappointed, I didn't find Joe cute at all. However, he was excited and happy that I was his pretend wife. I can still see his big toothy grin smiling at me.

Gerard would play our son and a little Black girl would be our daughter. In role play we never mixed races, unless there were not enough Black children in the class that day. If that did occur, a White one would be a child, never a spouse. l was so upset about Joe being my husband, I wouldn't participate in the role play. The teacher sent me to my seat. Joe looked so disappointed as well as the other two children. I was stubborn and had my perceptions of how I wanted things to go., which has always stayed with me.

We didn't live in the house in Compton very long. New Sheriffs were not put on patrol for two years. My father walked off his job because he wanted to be in the field, but they kept him on office duties. Later, he said he never wanted to be a Sheriff, he only applied because my mother encouraged it. He didn't think he'd be accepted, considering he was a Negro. My father left us and went back to Kansas where he grew up. While he was gone his sergeant came to our house to pick up my father's badge and gun, which were in the hall closet. My mother was a very beautiful woman.   She told me years later that the man had offered her a "job" as a call girl working for him. He said she could make a lot of money, since my father had left, he knew she could use it, considering our circumstances. He claimed to have clean White clients that would love a beautiful Colored girl like her. She politely told him no thanks, she'd be fine. My mother said the sergeant came by a couple of more times to try and convince her to work for him, but she refused and was very insulted.

We weren't fine, we were in big trouble.   My parents had purchased new furniture from an upscale department store when we moved into the new house. One day a large truck pulled up in front of our house without warning, picked up our still new furniture and took it away.   The cute boy Gerard was standing in front of our house and asked why they were taking our furniture? I lied, I was embarrassed, I said they had delivered the wrong furniture and was taking it back to get the right stuff.

My mother found a small job in a shirt factory that was not nearly enough to sustain us let alone pay the mortgage. Around Christmas she lost that job, however she got a temporary one with Mattel's the toy company. She scraped together enough money to buy my brother a bright blue racing car that we always saw on a T.V. commercial. There was a doll for me. I don't remember what my doll looked like, but I sure do remember that car.

Not being able to pay the mortgage, we moved to my grandparent's house. While we were there my mother would take us to a friend's who lived in Watts. My mother obtained another small job. She didn't want my grandmother to have to watch us while she worked. She felt we were enough of a burden. I enrolled in a school in the neighborhood where my mother's friend lived. I think I was in the 4th grade. My class was far behind the class I had been in at my last school. The top or smartest group was using third grade books I had used the semester before.

I told my teacher who looked perplexed and didn't know what to say. The other children in the group looked at me in surprise. I think there was a perception by that school district that these poor Black children in Watts were not as smart as other children. This held them intentionally back. When I told my mother, she and my grandmother decided I would go to school in my grandparents' school district, which was Black middle class. I was back on track with the right books for my grade.   Not long after, my mother went on welfare and she rented a small house in another part of town.

Our new neighborhood was predominately Black, located in South Central Los Angeles. There was a spattering of White kids at my school. A White boy in my class named Billy was a cute little chubby boy with blond hair that was a little too long, as crew cuts were in style.   Billy was the only White child in my class. We were having a Halloween Party and part of the festivities was to tell jokes and stories. A girl, Marilyn, told one about a White man, a Mexican man, and a Colored man. In this type of joke the Colored man was always the fool, the ignorant buffoon. After Marilyn told her joke the class broke out in a big laugh, all but the teacher.

Our teacher, a Black man asked for a volunteer to take some cookies next door to another teacher's class. Everyone, including Billy raised their hand, the teacher selected Billy. When Billy was gone our teacher told us as Negroes we should never tell these kinds of jokes about our race being foolish or ignorant. He explained that such jokes were a put down to our race and that we should be proud of who we were and to never forget it. I took what he said to heart, never forgetting that lesson, and I never told those kinds of jokes.   He also told us he sent Billy on the errand because

123

this was something we needed to hear, not Billy, as these jokes weren't told to make fun of his race. Our teacher was wrong, Billy should have heard this lesson as well. How else could he have learned not tell such jokes?

When I was about eleven we moved to what was called the West Side. Our neighborhood was a mixture of Black, White, and Hispanic families. We were all friends except Lorraine who was White, thirteen, and still in elementary school in a special education class. Lorraine's eyes were bugged, crossed, and she was mentally challenged, although we didn't call it that back then. Lorraine told us she wasn't allowed to play with the Colored kids and her mother told her not to show the Colored boys her panties. We had seen her in the alley with White boys, but we didn't know what they were doing. None of us wanted to hang out with her anyway, we thought she was weird. After a few years, the White families moved away as they usually do. The junior high and high school I attended were still mixed and I still had friends of different races, but at home my friends were Black.

As time went on there were more horrific sights on the television after Ruby Bridges. There were Black people being beaten, dogs being set on them, water hoses shot with so much force knocking people to the ground, causing them to roll down the streets, in faraway places like Detroit, Mississippi, and Alabama. When I was thirteen, four girls my age were killed from a bombing at a church in the South, I was stunned. This kind of thing didn't happen where I lived, not in Compton or Los Angeles. I heard about incidents of racists' remarks and things that the police did to Black people where I lived, but as a child I wasn't exposed to it to a point that I was personally affected.

Looking back to 1961 through 1968 I found there were 28 documentations of Black and White, women and men, civil rights activists who were murdered. The majority took place in Alabama and Mississippi. To this day I have no desire to visit either state. These were places I vowed I would never go.

John F. Kennedy, Robert E. Kennedy, Malcom X, and Martin Luther King, Jr., were assassinated during those turbulent times. Due to the Civil Rights Movement spearheaded by Martin Luther King, Jr's leadership, John F. Kennedy's, and Lyndon Baines Johnson's diligence to push equality through the Congress, The Civil Rights Act signed by Johnson was passed in 1964. With it came Affirmative Action giving minorities equal opportunities for education and employment. Although, I was fourteen the Civil Rights Act would greatly impact my life.

In 1965, came the Watts Riot in Los Angeles, which started a few miles from my grandparent's house. It erupted just west of Watts, but it was close enough to say it was Watts. After the riot started there were tanks rolling down our street with armed National Guards, although there was no rioting on the West Side where we lived. As I watched the riot on T.V., I could relate to the anger and frustration of the people running around, destroying property, stealing from store fronts. It was during that time I changed. The murders of Civil Rights workers, the four little girls bombed in a church, my memory of Ruby Bridges, the murder of John F. Kennedy, and so much more had an effect on me.

I started reading books; *Nigger* by Dick Gregory, *The Autobiography of Malcom X*, James Baldwin's *The Fire Next Time*, books by Louis Lomax (who was also on T.V.), and others. I followed closely the words of Malcom X, Huey P. Newton, Stokely Carmichael, and H. Rap Brown. I went to US meetings run by Maulana Ron Karenga, to my mother and grandparents' dismay. I cut my hair short and fashioned it into an Afro and then let it grow out large and full like

Angela Davis. I was not a devotee of Martin Luther King Jr. I wanted something to happen, something big, to put a stop to the injustices perpetrated on my people. I thought violence was the answer, I was longing, impressionable, young, and filled with the rhetoric of my heroes. My adherence to a violent revolution didn't last, there was a better way evidenced by Martin Luther King, Jr. The revolution never came.

My last year in high school I stayed with my grandparents while my mother and family moved to Pomona California. My mother was able to purchase a house through a special program for low income families. She needed a $200 down payment, which she received from my grandfather. The monthly mortgage would be $127, less than she was paying for a two-bedroom apartment for what was now the six of us. This house had three bedrooms and two bathrooms. It was a nice house in a mixed middleclass neighborhood. My mother enrolled in a nursing program offered to welfare mothers, she became a nurse's aide, and later an LVN, (Licensed Vocational Nurse).

As Blacks moved in, Whites moved out. One of the few Whites still living on our street lived next door. Their little boys played with my sister, but my mother had no contact with the parents, not so much as a wave. One day the woman came over with a large bag of used clothes and gave them to my mother. It was the first time they had spoken to each other. My mother took the bag, thanked her, and that night threw them in the trash. The woman was probably trying to be nice, but it was insulting to my mother. We did not need her old clothes. My mother said some White woman was always trying to give Black people their trash. The family moved a few months later. Jokingly, my mother said they moved because their sons was too attached to my sister, they might grow up and want to date her. This may have been a contributing factor in their move.

After I graduated from high school I moved reluctantly to Pomona to live with my mother and siblings. The year before, I still lived with my grandparents, but had to spend the summer in Pomona with my mother. I didn't like it in Pomona, I had never lived around mostly White people and their hostility was apparent when we walked down the streets or went to the local mall. Wearing my hair in an Afro didn't help.

When I moved home, I enrolled in Mt. SAC, a community college, which originally had been a mental hospital. I only stayed a short time, I didn't even finish the quarter. There was just a hand full of Black students at Mt. SAC. We stuck together when we were on breaks, sitting under a large tree we claimed as our territory. The White students didn't interact with me, in classes I was ignored. I enrolled in a Gymnastics Dance class and no one would offer to be my partner, I did my exercises alone. I was miserable. This was nothing like the schools I attended in Los Angeles, where I had friends of all races. I had never been ostracized before.

There was a school bus that went through the neighborhoods picking up students in the morning and dropping the off in the early evening. Only the Black students rode this bus, except an older White Instructor who looked to be in his 60s. He was also my councilor. Our bus driver never engaged in social conversation with us, he wouldn't even make eye contact. He was a young White guy who wore a military haircut and was very gruff. One morning, he lit into us, he was furious. He shouted that we were dirty and always left the bus a mess. He shouted we were a pack of animals, among other things. We just looked at him as if he had lost his mind, some even snickered. The Instructor didn't say anything, but his face looked upset. I thought it was at us and he was in agreement with the bus driver.

When we reached the college, he waited until the bus driver stormed off, which he usually did before the riders got off. The Instructor stopped us, he said that the driver shouldn't have spoken to us in that manner, it was his job to clean the bus. He apologized for the bus driver, saying he would take care of the problem, and this would never happen again.

That evening before the bus driver took off to drive us home he apologized. He said the Instructor was very angry about the way he spoke to us, calling us animals. The driver explained that he had been to Viet Nam, causing him to be too rough with us. He admitted that his job was in jeopardy. He just wanted us to clean up our trash. His apology seemed sincere considering his job was on the line and the Instructor was drilling a hole through him with his eyes. After that we picked up our trash and there were no more problems, at least not on the bus.

The defining moment for me leaving school and eventually moving back to Los Angeles was an incident in my history class. This Instructor was lecturing on the Civil War and proceeded to say that Negroes were better off as slaves. I was the only Black student in the class. I couldn't believe what I was hearing. I raised my hand to refute what he had said. He refused to call on me or even look at me. He kept talking about how badly off Negroes were without the comforts of slavery, having a place to live, and food to eat. I didn't know what to do, I felt hot, and sick to my stomach. A young White man sitting behind me started waving his hand, telling the Instructor he was wrong. He told the young man to be quiet. With that I got up and walked out. I never went back to that school. I didn't feel I had an option.

I went with another Black woman I knew to a job fair that was being held at a Black church. We both were hired by a hosiery plant with headquarters in the South. I am sure we were hired as the results of Affirmative Action. The people who spoke with us were clearly from the South, which caused me some concern. A test I was given which indicated I was ambidextrous, that was news to me. When we started work we found that we were the only Blacks. The Whites that worked there were openly hostile and rude.

The Black woman and I worked as a team boarding nylon tubes on columns of metal formed legs that went through a steam machine that shaped the stockings. Often, when we went on break, upon our return our finished stockings would be all messed up, sometimes wet from the water hoses used during the process. We'd have to start over, defective products and a low quantity counted against us. One day we had enough and the woman I was teamed with started spraying the women closest to our work station with water. They didn't say or do anything, just got out of the way and laughed. Whoever was tampering with our production stopped.

The day after Bobby Kennedy was assassinated, we were sitting in the lunch area outside taking a break. Several Whites were sitting across from us laughing and joking about how happy they were that Bobby Kennedy was killed. They could see the anger in my face as I glared in their direction. They just kept laughing. I hadn't come to terms with the death of John Kennedy in 1963 when I was in junior high school. Bobby Kennedy's death in 1968 was as painful to me as the President's. Many of us thought Bobby Kennedy would take over where the President had left off.

I quit working at the plant because I developed a rash from the stockings, which caused my fingers and hands to breakout. There was no compensation. I also had to pay for my own doctor; my grandfather paid it for me. I decided Pomona wasn't for me. I went back to my grandparents in L.A. I got a job at the telephone company and an apartment I shared with a friend. There were only three Black women in the telephone company department where I worked. We handled teletype operations for hospitals and hotels customer telephone charges. One of the Black women that worked with me was a supervisor. She also was attending college. I looked up to her and felt there would be opportunities for me as well.

Working in the teletype department was daunting, due to the manager. She appeared to be very fond of my supervisor and the other young Black woman. I supposed they was the type of Black women this manager approved. There was nothing Afrocentric about them. The manager made it very clear that she didn't like me. I was the only one with an Afro and I didn't wear much makeup, unlike the others. The manager had a habit of coming by my chair at the switchboard, asking me questions about my hair, why I didn't wear it like the other girls, what did my hair that way mean? She also had a habit of patting my hair, which infuriated me. I could only cringe and try to move my head.

One of our duties was to take turns sending rubber bands in a canister up a vacuum tube to the floor above, where they made out the tickets to do the teletype orders. I didn't understand how this whole process of sending the rubber bands worked. On the floor above, someone would put rubber bands around the tickets and then put them into a canister that had a hole on two sides. The canister was put in the vacuum tube and sent down to my floor. The floor above had run out of rubber bands and asked us to send some back. When I was told to send them, I just placed them in the canister and away they went. After several hours of not receiving any tickets, it was found that the vacuum tube was stacked with canisters, that were stuck. When I sent my canister up I was supposed to put the rubber bands in an envelope first. The rubber bands were sucked from the canister holes and formed a block, preventing any canisters from coming through. A technician had to cut through the tube to release the canisters.

When the manager found out what caused the problem and who caused it, she stomped over to my chair. In front of everyone she screamed at me how stupid I was, how much production I had stopped, how much money I had cost the company. She went on and on, I tried to tell her I didn't know how I was supposed to send the rubber bands, no one had told me. She just kept on hollering and finally told me I would probably lose my job.

The next day when I came to work our Union Representative, an older White woman, asked to speak with me in the break room. She never smiled and always wore a white lace blouse and a black wool skirt, as if it were a uniform. She had grey almost white hair worn in a style like the 1940's. I was afraid she was going to tell me I was fired. Instead, she said she had filed a grievance on my behalf regarding what had taken place with our manager. Her role as my Union Rep., among other things, was to protect me from harassment by management. She gave me her home number and said to call if anything else like that happened that she didn't observe.

After the grievance was filed the manager called me into her office with the Union Rep. and apologized. She no longer stopped by my chair or spoke to me, but she got back at me in another way that the Union Rep couldn't do anything about. The department had different shifts. Initially, I worked 8:00 a.m. to 5:00 p.m. My shift changed to 6:00 a.m. to 3:00 p.m. I lived over an hour away by bus. I was always late and of course in trouble with a warning of termination. My new supervisor on this shift was a 60ish White woman named Mary, who sat down next to me one day. She told me that she and the Union Rep. had discussed what was going on with me and that they would do everything they could to protect me, as I was a good worker. I was surprised: now two White women were coming to my aid. Mary asked for my phone number, so she could call me every morning at 4:30 a.m. to wake me up. Mary's calls were a God send, I was no longer late for work. I so appreciated her help and kindness.

Being on time didn't stop the manager. My shift was changed again to nights. If you got off at 12:00 a.m. the telephone company provided you with a cab home. My shift ended at 11:00 p.m., no cab. I had to take the bus, arriving home well after 12:00 a.m. I was terrified and would run the five blocks home to my apartment. Occasionally, my aunt, a nurse who worked at a hospital not far from my job, would give me a ride if her shift coincided with mine, but usually I was on my own. Mary was no longer my supervisor and there was nothing she or the Union Rep. could do about shift assignments. I couldn't take it any longer, I looked for another job.

I got a position at a bank as a loan clerk. The now defunct bank was located in Baldwin Hills, where many Black celebrities and athletes lived. Some were customers at my bank. Our branch manager was named Jefferson Jergerson and he was the classic stereotype of a Southern White racist. I was one of two Blacks this time and I was still wearing that Afro. Whenever he looked in my direction he had a scroll. The only time he spoke to me was to tell me I had done something wrong. I overheard him once tell another manager that if the other Black girl did whatever she had done that he didn't like he would "kick her black ass." I stayed as far away from him as possible. He loved it when the famous Black football players came into the office. He'd always go over to them, invite them to sit at his desk with a cup of coffee, and talk football. His son was in high school and was a football player with hopes of going professional.

I didn't like working at this bank and decided to sign up with an employment agency. I was given a series of tests and they found that my skills were applicable to banking. The owner of the agency met with me after my tests. She told me they were impressive. She placed me with another bank where I was hired as a teller. I stayed for over twenty years, rising in the ranks. Occasionally, she would call about a job that may be of interest, but I was happy at the bank and never went on any interviews.

It was 1971, I was twenty-one. The bank where I was hired was in the garment district. My co-workers were very friendly, as well as the customers. Again, most of the people I worked with were Whites. There were two other Black women who worked with me on the teller line as tellers. They had little to do with me. Someone told me they overheard them saying I talked like a White girl, that I was always up in the White girls' faces, kissing the asses of my White customers. I liked my customers who frequently gave me items from their showrooms. Some would stand in my line waiting for me, even if another window was free. It wasn't because I kissed their asses, it was because I was very fast, more than competent, and pleasant. My personality and work ethic led to a promotion as Chief Teller in less than a year. Of course, that didn't help much with the two women, but they lightened up a little. They started speaking to me and sometimes engaged in minimal conversations, but still stayed at a distance.

I spoke the way everyone in my family spoke and like the kids at most of my schools. My mother didn't allow improper English, maybe that was the reason I didn't speak Ebonics, or much slang. Because the two Black women were not interested in my friendship, the other girls were. My friends where two Whites, a Hispanic, and a Japanese American girl. We were as thick as thieves. I participated in the Hispanic girl's wedding. I stood at the church entrance and directed people to sign her wedding book. I did get some quizzical looks, I was the only Black person there. One of my friends who looked just like a famous actress was my closest friend. We talked about trying to open a secondhand store. Although, I haven't seen her in years, we occasionally talk on the phone or via email and social media. Since 1971, she has always sent me a birthday card. I will admit that sometimes mine gets to her a little late.

After working as a teller for a couple of years, I saw there was an opening in the Wire Services Department, which would be another promotion. Thanks to the job I had at the telephone company in the teletype department I got the position. I transferred to the bank's service center, still in downtown L.A. I learned so much about moving money around the world and about computers. My new supervisor, a Jewish man, took me under his wing and taught me a great deal outside of my normal duties. Later, in the 1990's we both went to California Banking School as neither of us had degrees. Eventually, we became Vice Presidents. He was my dearest friend, we ate lunch together, socialized together. He was a genius with a great sense of humor. When he married his wife, who is Black, the three of us would go on day-trips in California and on trips to Las Vegas. She became one of my dearest friends as well. He and I remained close after I left the bank, until he passed away a few years ago.

During the 70's while I was working, I also attended night classes at a city college. It was always my intention to get a degree after I left Mt. SAC. I majored in finance, but I took classes in African American History as electives. Before college I was only taught about the Civil War, a soft tale of slavery, Harriet Tubman, and Booker T. Washington. There was a plethora of Black History and the Harlem Renaissance that fuelled my awareness and my desire to be a writer. I read books by Richard Wright, W.E.B. Dubose, and Langston Hughes to name a few. I was always an avid reader but, did not know about Black writers except through the books I read during my Black militant period. In high school, I enrolled and thoroughly enjoyed American and English Literature, although these classes did not include the works of Black writers. It was my secret desire to be a writer. When I was in my late 50s I enrolled into a Creative Writing Program at UCLA, receiving a Certificate with Honors. I have had some success with my writing.

In the late 80's my daughter and I moved from Los Angeles to Moreno Valley California, some 60 miles east of Los Angeles. I ran into a childhood friend who had moved there. She told me how nice it was and that mortgages were very affordable. I visited her many times and looked at several model homes until I found the right one. It had four bedrooms, two baths, a huge yard, and it was brand new. I kept my job in L.A. making the 60-mile commute. This was hard on my daughter as I was gone so much of the time, but this was the only place I could afford to buy a house. I didn't need all the space, but years later when the grandchildren came for visits, I was thankful I had purchased such a large home.

Moreno Valley was a culture shock. The population was 18,000, now it is over 207,000. When I first moved here it was mostly White. It was not uncommon to see a Confederate flag flying from someone's porch. When I moved to Moreno Valley it was during the time that Denny's had their discrimination scandal. I had taken my daughter there for dinner for the first time. When I ordered our meal the White waitress (that was all there were) gave me my bill before I received my food. I didn't understand because this was not normal. I asked her why I was paying now? With a stone face, she said that was their policy, so I paid her. Later I learned what was going on. Denny's only made Black patrons pay first, for which they were sued and lost.

During the Rodney King riot in Los Angeles in 1992, my White neighbors who lived across the street were very friendly. They said my daughter and I could stay at their house if we were afraid.

There was nothing for us to be afraid of and nothing was going on in Moreno Valley. I did appreciate the misplaced gesture. Over the years the White population diminished to 41%, displaced by Hispanics that make up 54%, the remainder is Black and others. Getting a job in Moreno Valley has always been difficult for Blacks. Several warehouses have opened here, which has been a positive impact. Opening a business, which my daughter has done, is also an option.

Having worked in financial institutions and achieving the level of Vice President, without a college degree other than California Banking School, and a Creative Writing Certificate from UCLA, I continued to have very few Black counterparts on my jobs. Affirmative Action opened the door, but only ajar. I have been retired for almost a decade and I wonder if that has changed. The current racist climate that has resurfaced after the 2016 election is extremely disturbing and appears to be getting worst in that racist and bigots feel empowered.

This open racism has rekindled some of my feelings from the 60's. I no longer advocate violence, but I do feel anger. Why are we going through this again, not just Blacks, but Hispanics, Jews, Muslims, LGBT, anyone who doesn't fit the idiocy of White Supremacy, the Nazim agenda, or fake Christians. Today, I also see an outrage in Whites that was not as apparent during the 60's. The Whites were not as vocal and active as they are now regarding racism, bigotry and injustice. As decent well-meaning and carrying people we RESIST and will put our country back on the right path.

Imogen Gladman on the 2018 Booker Prize Longlist

One of the most highly anticipated events of the cultural calendar is the announcement of the Booker Prize winner in October. The Booker Prize was first awarded in 1969, and has survived controversies over everything from the choice of judges to the decision in 2013 to allow submissions from the USA. This year, for the first time, entries from Ireland have been permitted. The prize aims to reward exceptional literary talent and this year's longlist (The Booker 'Dozen'), announced on 23rd July, comprises 13 titles. Six of the longlisted authors are from the UK, and two from Ireland. The list is determinedly Western-focused, with the remaining authors coming from the USA and Canada.

Refreshingly, some would say, middle-aged, middle-class white male heavyweights such as Julian Barnes and Alan Hollinghurst, who might have been expected to make the list, were largely eschewed in favour of less well-known names. The most well-known nominees are Michael Ondaatje (best known for *The English Patient*) who is in on the list with a historical novel, *Warlight*, and Richard Powers, whose environmentally-themed novel *The Overstory* has also earned a place on the list.

For the first time, the list includes a graphic novel, *Sabrina,* which has attracted much media attention, apparently to the discomfort of its writer, Nick Drnaso. Andrew Holgate, the literary editor of the Sunday Times, has recently declared the Booker "bust", and he is one critic to oppose Drnaso's inclusion. He feels that in including *Sabrina* on the longlist "you may as well include film or play scripts, or libretti. Books that are predominantly pictorial are a different art form." Others disagree, and assert that *Sabrina* is effectively a work of literary fiction, in graphic novel form. No doubt the debate will rumble on. It will be interesting to see whether graphic novels will make it onto subsequent lists. For my part, I'd love to see a short story collection make a future list: Google tells me this hasn't been the case since the inclusion of Alice Munro's *The Beggar Maid* in 1980.

I found the inclusion on the list of *Snap* by Belinda Bauer more startling. I was surprised to see a piece of genre crime fiction on the longlist. I found it entertaining and even funny in places - a fantastic holiday read, but I'll be stunned if it has made the grade to be included on the shortlist. I suspect Val McDermid's role of Booker judge this year has influenced its inclusion on the list – she has publicly endorsed the book as the best work of crime fiction she's read for some time. Some people I've spoken to have questioned her appointment as a judge at all, though she's an Oxford-educated, extremely commercially successful writer.

The list contains four debut novelists. One of these is Scottish poet Robin Robertson. His *The Long Take* is a genre-bending mixture of prose and verse, featuring an ex-soldier struggling with post-traumatic stress disorder after fighting in the Second World War, and trying to make his way in a filmic, noir post-war America. The imagery and writing are consistently beautiful, but the America it conjures up is unrelentingly bleak. Contemporary America isn't described any more positively: *The Mars Room* by established author Rachel Kushner is set in the US female prison system. Although lightened in places by bleak humour, it veers close to becoming a polemic. This work is a confidently composed state of the nation novel.

Daisy Johnson, born in 1990, is a young debut novelist, listed for *Everything Under*. Her previous, much-lauded work *Fen* was a collection of short stories, which is strange and beautiful, and conjures up a contemporary world, set in the fens, in which her largely female protagonists inhabit worlds that are strangely Gothic or reminiscent of ancient folk tales. She's definitely one to watch. Irish author Sally Rooney, also still in her 20s, attracted commercial success and widespread praise for her Dublin-set first novel *Conversations with Friends*, which seems destined to become a book club favourite (and is, in fact, under discussion by my own book club in September!). Her longlisted novel *Normal People* has just been published, and has received glowing reviews from many of those who were lucky enough to read advance copies.

Guy Gunaratne's *In Our Mad and Furious City*, another debut novel, focuses on a London housing estate as it explodes into race riots. One of the younger characters, Selvon, shares a name with Sam Selvon, the Trinidadian author of the excellent 1950s Windrush-generation novella *The Lonely Londoners*. That book had its bleak undercurrents but was lightened by humour and a bouncy optimism. For Gunaratne, hope has faded: his London, the London of now, is a dystopia, with "plastered-over billboards, ads that sold dreams for other people", and his rhythmical prose vividly evokes the urban environment in which his characters live. Gunaratne handles multiple narratives with panache, and this timely work is among my personal favourites.

Although I may not concur with all the judges' choices, I find the Booker longlist always offers an intriguing selection of literary fiction to temporarily slake my appetite for new and engaging fiction. After many years of longlist reading, I remain engaged in following the prize, and I'm looking forward to the announcement of the shortlist on 20th September and the overall winner on 16th October.

Segments

A Lizard in my Bra: A Memoir by Samantha Maw

I
'I love my wife, but she has an odour problem.'

I clutched the Red Pepper Newspaper in my sweaty, ink-stained fingers while travelling down the road from Entebbe airport towards Kampala. Travelling at lip-quivering speed and feeling somewhat fragile, I smiled at the bizarre article. Not only because it was a little too much information, but also because it reminded me that from now on my world had changed. Frank had met me in arrivals that morning with an energetic smile and a piece of crumpled cardboard reminding me who I was.

"Ah Teacher Samantha, you have reached! You are so welcome!"

I had met Frank earlier that year when I had visited *Asiimwe College of Excellence*. He was a member of the ground staff and a genuinely good human being. The sort that was always around to solve any problem and make you feel better about life in general. However, at that particular time, even Frank's jolly disposition couldn't settle my nerves.

I had visited Kampala 6 months previously with some friends who worked at the college, and they introduced me to the Principal. We had discussed the possibility of me spending some time there teaching and after deciding to quit my job as a Secondary school R.E. Teacher in Lincolnshire, here I was, doing what I had always dreamed about. I was finally in Africa.

My anxiety threatened to get the better of me but crying in front of Frank would confuse and probably alarm him, so I tried to focus on the article. `You must advise your wife that there will be no relations of a sexual nature unless she attends to her personal hygiene,` Dr Dembe wrote. I had been wearing the same clothes for more than 24 hours, and I smelt like a Baboon's armpit. Clearly, there would be no relations of a sexual nature for me either.

"I can't believe you are finally here! I never thought you'd make it!" shouted inner-monologue-lady (does anyone else have one of those?). For word economy, she will henceforth be known as Imla. Imla and I go back a long way. She has always been quite feisty and to this day views herself and her commentary on my daily life as indispensable. I questioned her lack of confidence in me as Frank careered down the wrong side of the road to miss some cows.

I *had* made it to Uganda all by myself, and this thought caused the panic to dissipate a little. 4,000 miles of dragging cases; being screened for illegal substances; enduring incomprehensible flight entertainment, eating processed food and making frequent trips to the toilet to sample the hand cream. Just a small travel tip for the uninitiated - never use the plane toilet without shoes. The floor was damp, and my socks became suspiciously moist. My naked thighs also experienced the horrors of a liberal toilet seat sprinkling.

The journey had taken 24 hours, with a four-hour change-over in Dubai. Hours of being squashed between two blanket covered human mountains. Every square inch of the plane was crammed tightly with bodies and luggage, and I had been allocated the dreaded middle seat. Moving any part of my body had been difficult, and because the blanket-mountains had slept the whole way, I found myself having to perform impressive acrobatics to reach the aisle. I was concerned one of them might wake up to find my butt in their face. The stress got to me at one point and I choked on my Murray mint, swallowing it whole. As my airway began to close, I wondered if any of the flight attendants had performed the Heimlich Manoeuvre on a passenger before. Fortunately, the offending mint managed to dislodge itself without assistance, and I finally started to relax.

The road from Entebbe to Kampala had a charming, reckless beauty that made my heart beat faster. It was covered in cavernous potholes and faded road markings, and the soil each side was a baked orange colour. Banana trees and palms nestled amongst small rustic shops and market stalls, created from corrugated tin sheeting and shipping containers. There was a hefty police presence; military pickup trucks parked up every mile or so with uniformed men brandishing automatic rifles. There were crowds of people moving between the traffic with cows and goats; chickens scattering noisily in all directions; barefooted children with babies on their backs shouting, "Hallo Muzungu!!"[1] and waving excitedly; countless scooters racing by with all sorts of seemingly impossible items stacked behind the rider: front doors; three-seater sofas; metres of lead piping; perplexed looking goats.

This was the beginning of my great adventure.

II
The Only Muzungu in the Village

Two days later, after spending some time with the Principal and his family in his palatial house in the mountains, Frank dropped me off at my apartment in Mbuya. I had a couple of weeks to settle in before the term started. It was the middle apartment of three and each one had a small front garden. My place had a well-established avocado tree growing in front of a colonial style veranda. The front door led into a white-tiled open living space, with some very elaborate black metal work furniture and an open plan kitchen area with space for a cooker and fridge. Down a small corridor on the right was the master bedroom; overshadowed by a set of dark heavy wooden built in wardrobes, hanging at a bit of an angle. Off to the left was the main wet room, tiled from floor to ceiling, and the end of the corridor there was a second bedroom.

"You're going to rattle around in this place. Good luck washing the floor." Imla quipped.

"It's going to be just fine. I'm here, and it's all going to be just FINE."

I was feeling a little bit homesick and wobbly again. For someone who suffers from anxiety, the whole giving-up-everything-and-moving-to-Africa was an interesting life choice.

"Pull yourself together!" chelped Imla. "Try to keep up the pretence of being adventurous for at least the first week."

"But what if it's all been a terrible mistake?"

I felt snot bubbling in my nose.

"Well, you've no one to blame but yourself."

A high wall surrounded the apartment block, secured by a large, blue steel gate with two deadbolts and a padlock. The apartment itself had swirly iron bars at the windows, and the door was in two parts: a metal door resembling the gate, locked with a padlock and bolted from the inside, and then a swirly iron frame, also with a padlock. The bolts were always a bit stiff and made a

---

[1] Muzungu or Mzungu is an East African term referring to a white traveller. Its literal meaning is `someone who wanders around without purpose.`

screeching noise every time you pulled them across. It became a very familiar sound (it was like living in a high-security prison) and you couldn't leave or exit in a hurry.

On the right lived a Ugandan couple with a baby and a maid, on my left a Turkish businessman called Tarkan. The couple relied on their maid to open the gate, whatever time of day or night it was. At 3 am I would hear the car pull up outside, the engine grumbling intrusively, and the husband would honk his horn loudly several times until most of the village had woken up. Everyone in Kampala who could afford it had a guard or a maid whose responsibility it was to open up for the householder, but in my compound the process seemed to take forever. One night I became so mad I marched out, opened the gate myself, and then yelled something unsavoury to the driver.

It's odd how you assume that the rules you grow up within your own country are applicable everywhere. Take the noise curfew, for example. Tell someone in Uganda they can't make noise after 11 pm in a residential area and they will look at you with confusion. Your party is judged on how big your PA system is and how many miles the decibels can travel.

Morning hours weren't sacred either. If it wasn't the cockerel next door that woke me up at 4 am, it was the local primary school bell. Or the call to prayer. Or the women next door sweeping and sharing jokes. One morning it was a pair of Marabou stalks arguing like old men. This particular breed of bird had definitely been last in line when it came to good looks; four feet of mite ridden plumage, a grotesque boat-like beak topped with wild beady eyes and a small bald head. I knocked on the window, and they spread out their vast wings and bandy legs and glided off to horrify someone else.

Despite the late night honking, the PA systems and ugly wildlife, my new world became increasingly delightful and fascinating.

Outside the compound, banana, paw-paw and jackfruit trees gave shade to women shelling peanuts, children washing from bowls, and men bent over their motorbikes sleeping. Other women sat outside small single-roomed houses with a curtain serving as a front door, boiling rice or matoke in a pan balanced on a makeshift fire. Clean washing was slung over fences and hedges to dry. The local shops were small huts with a random selection of presumed essentials: peppers, onions, bogoya[2], string, jerry cans, milk, airtime, brushes, matches, and gin or vodka in a bag (it was almost cheaper than water). The shop I often went to was managed by a lady my age who seemed to spend her whole time watching US prosperity sermons. It was good to be regularly reminded that God wanted me to be rich, and all I had to do to achieve this was send 25 dollars into the Apocalypse Healing Centre in Michigan.

Where the village path met the main road, there was a bar with a TV fixed to the wall. I say wall, but what I really mean is a collection of plywood stapled together. There was also a pool table and a short man in a brown bobble hat selling Nile Special and Bell Lager. The roof was corrugated metal, supported by a wooden post at each corner. There was often a match on TV, watched by men in old Arsenal and Man U shirts. Local hip-hop music crackled through old speakers, and when I passed, I usually got accosted in some way.

"Ahh Muzungu, you're my style! Let me try you on for size!"

It wasn't too long before my polite, but awkward smile was replaced with a scowl and a mildly offensive hand gesture. I think we eventually came to an understanding.

---

[2] Bogoya is the collective name for the yellow, large bananas grown in Uganda.

Sometimes, if I needed to go further afield, I took a Boda Boda[3] from the Stage opposite the Bar (stage meaning rank or stand). This stage consisted of a line of about eight motorbikes straddled by their drivers. They would loudly compete for business, and I would stand and wait until they decided whose turn it was to take me and at what cost. It was very exhilarating – sat behind a sweaty stranger, gripping the seat with my thighs, hair flying, dust in my eyes, sailing over potholes. One false move and I could end up arse over elbow; a pile of bloody, bruised limbs in a ditch in the middle of nowhere.

"Oh, for goodness sake, stop exaggerating!"

"I'm not Imla – it was a genuine possibility!"

"Why did you keep taking the risk then?"

"I didn't think I had a choice. I just went with it..."

I guess that's always been my problem.

3.

The Juice of Enthusiasm

The first morning I was due to be at the College, I woke up to find a large pig in my backyard. It was meandering in and out of the bed sheets I had hung out the night before. I lived in a closed compound, so I couldn't understand where it had come from. Our eyes met, and it regarded me with some menace. Were pigs in Uganda violent? A headline quickly ran through my head. MUZUNGU TEACHER BORED TO DEATH BY RABID PIG. I clanged the back door shut. I never saw the beast again and have since wondered whether the anti-malarial drugs had pig visions as a side effect.

It was too hot to walk, so I decided to get a Matatu[4]. The attendant ushered me inside with a despondent grunt, and I tentatively stepped over a rolled-up carpet, two live chickens in a bucket and a large lady wearing a very brightly coloured Gomesi[5]. She had a small girl on her lap. There was no space on the floor under my seat due to a drinks crate, so once I had squeezed my rather large bottom into the unreasonably small space, I had to put my legs up so that my knees were almost touching my cheekbones (particularly unfortunate as I was wearing a skirt). The sweat ran into my eyes, and the smell of distressed chicken made me want to gag. I smiled inanely at the small child next to me who was poking me and pulling my ponytail.

`This is your dream, remember! ` Imla was quick to point out.

I did my best to ignore her.

After shouting, `Masao` (Luganda for stop) and creating a riot of laughter in the bus, I managed to extricate myself from the vehicle and pay my dues.

The path that sloped down past the primary section and into the College had a couple of shiny SUV's filled with luggage parked up on the grass verge. As I got closer to the college gates, a parent was having a loud, heated discussion with one of the security guards. In front of the College

---

[3] Boda Boda is an East African term for a motorcycle taxi. It is thought to originate from the fact that you could cross country borders on one of these without having to supply the necessary paperwork.

[4] East African term for a 14-seater minibus taxi. All Matatus in Kampala are white with blue dashes along the side. They usually have a religious motto on the back window such as `Love Jesus` or `Allah is Merciful`.

[5] A Gomesi is a floor-length colourful dress woman wear in southern Uganda, with huge sleeves and a wide belt.

gates, there was a mountain of cement, and a large steel drum of boiling tar. A man in a t-shirt and slacks was poking the boiling asphalt with a big stick, steam spiralling around his face. I managed to squeeze past the drum of death and headed off to the dining hall for training.

The dining room was full of wooden benches and doubled up as a theatre, as it had a large stage at the back. I, however, didn't have to sit on the benches as the Headteacher had gone to the trouble of getting me a `special chair`. It was high backed and had a red velvet seat. I was very grateful, but it did make me look like a visiting Bishop, which was a bit awkward. The staff were extremely smart and very welcoming, and I liked them all immediately. It didn't take me long to clock a broad-shouldered man with very dark skin who was moving about the staff, greeting them and filling in a register. I saw him from behind at first and waited eagerly for him to turn around. When he did, his soft eyes and broad smile stalled me.

"Close your mouth, you're looking desperate," Imla said with disgust.

"Quiet, Imla. I think I might have just met the man I am going to marry."

I asked the lady next to me (an English Teacher called Ranya) who he was.

"That's Teacher Aakil. He is head of Maths but is also in the Senior Leadership Team."

"Seems nice," I said, trying to appear nonchalant. But in an instant, I had become an advocate of the love at first sight theory. There must be something in that because later I did grow to love him very much.

After lots of milky tea and some banana pancakes, the training started. We all had to introduce ourselves, and I was asked to share my marital status. I felt a little bit like a contestant on a dating game show. When I said I was single all the men cheered, including Aakil. I gave him my best coy smile and undid the top button on my shirt.

During the first session, we looked at how to cope with stress, conflict, uncontrollable anger.

"Very appropriate in your case, remember when you…."

"Shhh, Imla, I need to concentrate!"

I listened carefully, although it sparked in me a sense of foreboding. My temper had, on occasion, got the better of me. Apparently, if I was overcome with any negative feelings, I could pray to God, consider myself lucky, and take a cold shower. There were, of course, the usual references to talking about your feelings and planning your time wisely.

The Principal also gave a talk on Attitude vs Output. You can tell if I am enjoying something because I will make lots of notes, and on this occasion, my pen was flying. He talked about having the juice of enthusiasm flowing through your veins at all times, regardless of the circumstances. I needed to ask myself each day whether my juices were in full flow or whether I had let negativity suck them out of me.

"Ask yourself in private though," said Imla, "as it could lead to some misunderstanding."

When talking about developing good relationships with the students, the Principal used the Art teacher as an example. He listed the reasons why she had been so successful at this over the last year and then encouraged the other teachers would give her a special celebratory clap. This consisted of two long claps and three short ones. I had even been noticed as someone who had demonstrated the `juice` of enthusiasm (although I was too new to get a celebratory clap).

"Wait until they get to know you. Then they will realise it`s all an act," said Imla.

I couldn't disagree.

It wasn't just all praise and rhythmic clapping. The teachers were asked to think of a colleague who had done something annoying and unhelpful during the last term. They went on to openly discuss this in front of the whole group.

"Teacher Juliet is always late for duty!"

"Teacher David steals chairs from my classroom and forgets to put them back."

"Teacher Amira slurps her tea!"

Profuse apologies from the named offenders followed and everyone seemed to take it in good faith, before the next topic was introduced.

"I don't like the way you always forget something when you leave the house," said Imla. "And when you squeeze the toothpaste from the middle."

"Shh, Imla I am trying to concentrate. The Principal is now talking about what to do when I start vomiting and having hallucinations. "

In the afternoon I had the chance to explore the school grounds. Both the junior and senior school were built into a hillside so everywhere was either a climb or a descent. The junior school was a collection of rectangular buildings with metal framed windows and doors and blue corrugated tin roofs. Each classroom was painted in two colours, brown on the bottom and cream on the top, inside and out. The international curriculum classrooms were white and blue to reflect the new uniform. There were also rows of dorms and a large block of staff apartments. The campus was a myriad of ochre stone paths, ditches, steps and smartly clipped bushes. There were signs giving instructions like, `Keep the Sch Clean` and, `You Rest You Rust`. At the foot of the junior campus, there was a small swimming pool, and a gargantuan playing field lined with Banana and Eucalyptus trees. I had been advised that it was common to see Vervet monkeys on campus, so if I had food on me, I needed to keep it well hidden.

The secondary campus was similar but much more extensive. The gate welcomed you in several languages, and a sign painted in blue on the wall said, `Education that strives for Excellence`. A small stream ran between the two campuses, through a wooded area that supposedly contained snakes. As you walked up the main path, there were well-manicured lawns and explosions of green, red and orange foliage against the bright blue sky. In the middle of one lawn stood a large circular piece of metal suspended from a free-standing iron frame – the school bell. If you took the path to the left, it would take you to the main reception building; the school bus parked up in front. To the right of the reception and up some metal stairs was the assembly hall and dining room, and if you walked around the back of the building, you saw the kitchen on the left and the staff toilet up on a high stone ledge. It was quite a climb. The door was made up of several planks that didn't quite reach the top, or bottom, so at least plenty of light was allowed in. There was a porcelain long drop inside – two ridged areas each side of the hole where you could put your feet. There was also, unexpectedly, a flushing mechanism. While still lingering over the porcelain on my first visit, I tugged at the chain.

"Next time remember to jump out of the way to avoid splashback," Imla advised.

Back on the main path, if you continued upwards, you passed the classrooms, the dormitories and eventually the staff quarters. This was a small cluster of basic three-roomed houses; an open plan living room, two bedrooms and a small toilet. Most rooms had concrete floors with pieces of carpet here and there. Some had a kitchen area, but most of the teachers had maids who did their cooking and washing out on the porch. I felt a bit guilty about my large apartment and thought perhaps I should have accepted a house on site. But I just couldn't get used to the idea of not having a bathroom and a kitchen. At that time, it was just a step further than I was prepared to go. I had always been a bit spoilt, and Uganda was yet to work its magic on me.

Looking back now, jetting off to Africa was rather a rash thing to do, especially when I had a mortgage and a secure job. The effects were more far-reaching than I could have imagined at the time, but then I wonder if we would take any risks at all in life at all if we knew what was around the corner. I planned to stay out in Uganda for a year but ended up there for four amazing, frustrating, rewarding, and hot years. In that time, I worked in three schools (both as a volunteer and employee), lived in three different houses, fell in love, had my heart broken, and had several near-death experiences. I went to Uganda as one person and came back another. A fact that didn't go unnoticed by my dad, who looked at me over breakfast one dreary Tuesday morning back in Lincolnshire and said,

"It's like you're some kind of alien now."

I am sure he meant well.

Disclaimer & Acknowledgements

I have tried to recreate events, locales and conversations from my memories of them. In order to maintain anonymity, I have changed the names of individuals and places. I may have changed some identifying characteristics and details such as physical properties, occupations and places of residence. I have also, on occasion, overdramatised actual events for your reading pleasure.

The College mentioned has gone from strength to strength over recent years, and currently enjoys an excellent reputation. It offers an impressive range of local and international qualifications and a modern, high-tech learning environment. It was an absolute pleasure to be part of the team, and I learnt much more than I taught anyone else during my time there. I will always be profoundly grateful for the experience and Uganda itself has contributed greatly to the person I am now.

Biographies of Contributors

Shirley Bell has been the poetry editor and the editor in chief of *The Blue Nib* since 2017. She is a widely published and anthologised poet as well as an experienced workshop tutor and writer-in-residence. Her poetry is archived in the Special Collection in the University of Lincoln's Library and as a result, she has collected together all her published poetry from 1982 to early 2016 in her book, *Dark is a Way and Light is a Place.* She has been writing poetry since the 1980s and has read widely all over the UK, including appearing at London's South Bank Centre and the Arvon Centres. She has been a Literature Consultant for Lincolnshire and Humberside Arts and edited their magazine, *Proof.* Her poetry has appeared in many magazines, and anthologies including Faber and Faber's *Poetry Introduction 6, Six the Versewagon Poetry Manual* and *Anvil New Poets,* which have featured large selections of her work. The Wide Skirt also published her pamphlet *Hanging Windows on the Dark.* Her latest collection, *The Still Room, new and selected poems chosen by Dave Kavanagh,* was published in 2018 under The Blue Nib imprint.

Arthur Broomfield is a poet, novelist, publisher and Beckett scholar from County Laois. His previous works include *When the Dust Settles* (International University Press), *The Poetry Reading at Semple Stadium* (Lapwing), *The Empty Too: Language and philosophy in the works of Samuel Beckett* (Cambridge Scholars' Publishing) and *Mice at the Threshing* (Lapwing). He is editor of the online poetry journal *Outburst* and delivers occasional lectures on the works of Samuel Beckett. *Cold Coffee at Emo Court* is his first full collection.

David Butler has published three novels, the most recent of which, *City of Dis* (New Island), was shortlisted for the Kerry Group Irish Novel of the Year, 2015. His second poetry collection, *All the Barbaric Glass*, was published in 2017 from Doire Press. Arlen House is to bring out his second short story collection in 2019. Literary prizes include the Maria Edgeworth (twice), ITT/Red Line and Fish International Award for the short story, the Scottish Community Drama, Cork Arts Theatre and British Theatre Challenge awards for drama, and the Féile Filíochta, Ted McNulty, Brendan Kennelly, Poetry Ireland/Trocaire, and Bailieborough awards for poetry.

Lyn Ann Byrne is a Communications Specialist and Business Trainer. She has also worked as a print and broadcast journalist and has contributed to various fiction and non-fiction publications including *The Bohemyth, HCE Review, thebluenib.com, The Irish Times, Women's Way, Irish Property buyer magazine, Anglers Digest and deafhear.ie.* She has an honours degree in Business and French, a master's degree in Journalism and studied creative writing in the richly historic eighteenth-century Carlow College. She has completed her first novel and is currently seeking representation.

Nora Cornell is a Minneapolis-based high school poet. She lives with her parents, younger brother, and four chickens. When not writing poems, she's a theater kid with a penchant for storytelling. Some of her influences include folk and fairy tales, poet Sarah Kay, and author Kelly Barnhill.

Bernie Crawford is from County Galway and is co-editor of the popular poetry newspaper *Skylight 47*. In 2017 she won first prize in the *Poetry Ireland/Trocaire* poetry competition. In 2018 she was shortlisted in the Fish Poetry Competition and in *Poems for Patience* competition. Her work has been published in many journals including *Mslexia, Crannog, Boyne Berries* among others and has appeared in a number of anthologies. She is currently working on her first collection.

Cathy Donelan is a writer from the west of Ireland. Her fiction has appeared in *ROPES, The Honest Ulsterman, Dodging The Rain, The Nottingham Review, Spontaneity, The Lamp Graduate Journal, Smoky Blue Literary and Arts Magazine* and A New Ulster's 2017 anthology The *Hidden and Divine: Female Voices in Ireland*. Her poetry has appeared in *The Galway Review, A New Ulster* and *The Blue Nib*. She has won the December 2015 Poetry Pulse Prize and been highly commended in the 2016 Fool For Poetry International Chapbook Competition.

Kate Ennals is a poet and writer and has published material in a range of literary and on line journals (*Crannog, Skylight 47, Honest Ulsterman, Anomaly, Burning Bush 2, Poets meets Politics, The International Lakeview Journal, Boyne Berries, North West Words* etc). Her first collection of poetry *At The Edge* was published in 2015. She has lived in Ireland for 25 years and currently runs poetry and writing workshops in County Cavan, and organises At The Edge, Cavan, a literary reading evening, funded by the Cavan Arts Office. Before doing an MA in Writing at NUI Galway in 2012, Kate worked in local government and the community sector for thirty years, supporting local groups to engage in local projects and initiatives. Her blog can be found at kateennals.com.

Molly Fennig grew up in St. Paul, Minnesota. Currently, she is pursuing a major in neuroscience (and minors in both Spanish and English) at Swarthmore College in Pennsylvania. Her work has also appeared in the *Widener Blue Route*.

Nathan Fidler lives in Nottingham, working as a copywriter while reviewing film and music in his spare time. He writes his own music under the moniker King Fringe and thinks of Bill Murray as his spirit guide

Imogen Gladman, Fiction Editor of *The Blue Nib*, is a knowledgeable editor with 20 years of professional experience. She has expertise and qualifications in the fields of literary fiction, French literature and culture, classical studies, history of art and linguistics amongst others. London based, she is well placed for contacts in literary and cultural circles. She also has a strong social media presence which we hope will help to grow and develop *The Blue Nib's* profile. Above all, she loves contemporary literary fiction, which she devours with endless enthusiasm. Imogen is looking forward to selecting fiction for *The Blue Nib*, and contributing reviews of books, theatre and other cultural events, along with articles and news items to the magazine and the online site.

Michael A. Griffith began writing poetry as he recovered from a disability-causing injury. His poems, essays, flash fiction and articles have appeared in many print and online publications and anthologies. He resides and teaches near Princeton, NJ. His first poetry chapbook is slated to appear later this year from *The Blue Nib*.

Stephen House: has had many plays commissioned and produced. He's won two Awgie Awards (Australian Writers Guild), The Rhonda Jancovic Poetry Award for Social Justice, Advertiser Best Playwright Prize & 2nd place in Poetry at Sawmillers Prize. He's been nominated for Patrick White & Queensland Premiers Drama Awards, Overland's Fair Australia Fiction Prize, a Greenroom Award for Best Actor and several poetry prizes. He's received Australia Council literature residencies to Canada and Ireland and an Asialink to India. He's been published by The Australian Script Center, Currency Press Australia, Australian Poetry Journal, grey borders magazine Canada, Third Street Writers USA, Burmingham Arts Journal USA, and many websites. Stephen is listing all his published poems on tablo. He's performed his poetic monologues widely, most recent - "Almost Face To Face" and "Appalling Behavior." Stephen identifies as a Queer Nomad and is devoted to full time travel, Yoga and his writing & performing and the environment.

Nigel Jarrett is a former newspaperman and a double prizewinner: the Rhys Davies Award for short fiction and, in 2016, the inaugural Templar Shorts award. His first story collection, *Funderland*, published by Parthian, was praised by the Guardian, the Independent, the Times and many others, and was longlisted for the Edge Hill Prize. His debut poetry collection, *Miners At The Quarry Pool*, also from Parthian, was described by Agenda poetry magazine as 'a virtuoso performance'. Jarrett's first novel, *Slowly Burning* (GG Books) was published in 2016, as was his second story collection, *Who Killed Emil Kreisler?* (Cultured Llama Publishing). Templar is about to publish his three-story pamphlet, *A Gloucester Trilogy*. Based in Monmouthshire, Jarrett writes for Jazz Journal, the Wales Arts Review, Arts Scene in Wales, Slightly Foxed, Acumen poetry magazine, and several others. His poetry, fiction, and essays appear widely. For many years he was a daily newspaper music critic, and now freelances in that capacity. When he can find time, he swims.

Derek Kannemeyer was born in Cape Town, South Africa, raised in London, England, and now lives and writes in Richmond, VA, in the USA, after marrying an American girl he met while living in France. (A recent genome test informs him that he is about 40% European, about 40% Asian, and about 20% African, so he may be of unsettled blood.) His writing has appeared in publications from *Fiction International* and *Rolling Stone* to (this year) *Chaleur, Bacopa Literary Review, Riddled With Arrows, River Heron, Aethlon,* and elsewhere. After winning the inaugural Blue Nib Chapbook Contest, he published a collection of light verse, *An Alphabestiary*.

Simran Keshwani is an India based author currently pursuing her Masters research in Sydney, Australia. Her literary career has been based on exploring the question of spaces - personal, private, public, closed, open, empty, hollow and full and how they interact viz-a-viz the performances of being in the 21st Century. Her first book, *Becoming Assiya*, explores the same questions from the perspective of a migrant.

Charles G Lauder, Jr is an American poet who has lived in a rural pocket of the UK for the past eighteen years. Dreams, politics, his Texas childhood, relationships, and family life dominate his poetry.

Emma Lee's most recent collection is *Ghosts in the Desert* (IDP, UK 2015), she co-edited *Over Land, Over Sea: poems for those seeking refuge* (Five Leaves, UK, 2015), reviews for *The High Window Journal, The Journal, London Grip and Sabotage Reviews* and blogs at http://emmalee1.wordpress.com.

Aurora M. Lewis is a retiree, having worked in financial institutions for over 40 years. In her late 50's she received a Certificate in Creative Writing-General Studies, with honors from UCLA. Aurora's poems, short stories, and nonfiction have been accepted by *The Literary Hatchet, Gemini Magazine, Persimmon Tree, Tinderbox Poetry Journal,* and *Jerry Jazz Magazine*, to name a few.

Roy Liran Born in Israel in 1971. Lives in the Galilee with his wife and twins. Works in the IAA (Israel Antiquities Authority) as an archaeologist, architect and artist. His first poetry book, *Not who I thought,* was published (in Hebrew) in 2016 by Pardes Publishing. It includes 65 poems and several drawings by the author.

Marissa McNamara: While Marissa McNamara writes about many topics, her current work revolves around her husband's death in 2004 when she was 35 and he was 42. She hopes to show the many facets of dealing with loss, especially those that are brutally honest. Marissa teaches English at Georgia State University and in local Atlanta prisons. She is also a contributing poetry editor for *The Chattahoochee Review*. Her work has appeared in several publications including the anthology *My Body My Words* and the journals *RATTLE, The Cortland Review*, and *Amsterdam Quarterly*. Marissa lives in Atlanta with her three crazy dogs, one very patient boyfriend, and a flock of pink plastic flamingos.

Samantha Maw is a teacher by profession who has recently completed her MA in Creative Writing at the University of Lincoln in the U.K. She is a member of Lincoln Creative Writers, Women in the Arts (WITA) and Outspoken Poets. She regularly performs at local and national Spoken Word events and dabbles in amateur dramatics. She is also a regular contributor to *The Blue Nib*.

Audrey Molloy was born in Dublin and grew up in rural Wexford. She now lives in Sydney, where she works as an optometrist and medical writer. Her poetry has recently appeared in *The Moth, Crannog, The Irish Times, Orbis, Meanjin, Cordite, Banshee* and *Popshot*. Audrey's work has been nominated for the Forward Prize and she is one of Eyewear Publishing's Best New British and Irish Poets 2018. She was runner up for the 2017 Moth Poetry Prize and has been shortlisted for several other awards. poetry www.audreymolloy.com

Jeremy Nathan Marks is an American living in London, Canada. Recent writing appears/is appearing in *The London Free Press, OTV Magazine, The Black Lion Journal, Chiron Review, Rat's Ass Review, Mojave River, The Wire's Dream, Unlikely Stories, Landlocked Lyres, Alien Pub, The Blue Hour IV*, and *The Wild Word*. His self-published poetry collection *Facebook Friend* will be published in July.

Tom Paine's poetry is upcoming or published in T*he Nation, Glasgow Review of Books, The Moth Magazine, Blackbox Manifold, Volt, Fence, Forklift, Ohio, Epiphany, The Common, Green Mountain Review, Tinderbox, Hunger Mountain, Hotel Amerika, Gulf Stream, Tampa Review, World Literature Today* and elsewhere. Stories have been published in *The New Yorker, Harper's, The New England Review, The Boston Review, Best New Southern Stories, The O. Henry Awards* and twice in the Pushcart Prize. He has won fellowships from Sewanee, Yaddo, and Bread Loaf, and written for Francis Ford Coppola. His first collection, *Scar Vegas* (Harcourt), was a New York Times Notable Book of the Year and a Pen/Hemingway finalist. He is an associate professor in the MFA program at the University of New Hampshire.

Ruth Quinlan lives in Galway, Ireland. She won the 2018 Galway University Hospital Arts Trust - Poems for Patience competition, the 2014 Over the Edge New Writer of the Year Award and the 2012 Hennessy Literary Award for First Fiction. She has also been shortlisted or runner-up for other competitions like Cúirt New Writing, Francis Ledwidge Poetry Awards, and Doolin Writers' Weekend. Her work has been published by the likes of the *Irish Independent, Crannóg, Skylight 47*, and has been nominated for the Forward Poetry Prize.

Polly Richardson (Munnelly) is a Dublin born poet now living and writing in Meath. She has been published both nationally and internationally in many anthologies and e-zine under the surname of Munnelly and more recently Richardson. She is member of Navan writers' group: The Bulls Arse and Cork based group Blackwater Poetry. Polly has been heard reading at open mic nights and festivals throughout Ireland including The Blackwater International poetry festival and on live links broadcasting internationally as part of the festival 2013, 2014, 2015 and 2016. Her poems have featured on their poetry trail in 2014 and 2016. She has also been heard reading at; The sunflower sessions, The Collective and Dublin writer's forum summer bash (2015 ,2016, 2017 and 2018) Good thyme Thursday sessions, Blackbird Books and 2016 she was part of the 'Awaken Your Soul' event that was short listed for a Sabator award in London 2017. In 2017 she travelled to Amsterdam and was heard reading in Harrlem alongside Frisian Poet Tsead Brunja as part of a collective gathering of poets and musicians. Some of her work has been published and appeared in the following outlets; *Irish based Solstice Initiative Poetry Journals; Connections in 2012, Aqueous 2013. US based Mad Swirl Poetry Forum* 2013 to 2016 where she is now a contributing poet. *Songs for Julia anthology*, Italian based e-zine *Lotus Eater, Blue max review, Poems for Fukushima anthology* and *Twenty Seven signs* anthology in 2014. *The Sea anthology* 2015, has work included in *Boyne Berries Anthology* celebrating poet Francis Ledwigs 100th centenary 2017. *Blue Nib e-zine* 2017 & 2018 including a honourable commendation in their Second Chapbook Contest by judge Kevin Higgins 2018, *Flare* 06 & 08 2018 and *Nixes Mate Review* Boston 2018. Her poem *Fox Thought* published by Mad Swirl was used as part of an initiative to inspire young artists in a local art school in Texas USA, inspiring incredible sculptures and drawings. And has two of her poems displayed on the poetry trail in Drogeda as part of Fleadh na hEireann 2018. She is currently working on her first collection.

Kenneth Robbins is the author of five published novels, 29 published plays, and numerous stories, essays, and memoirs. He is a past recipient of the Associated Writing Programs Novel Award and the Toni Morrison Prize for Fiction. The four poems featured are from his unpublished collection, *THE BOOK OF SLAUGHTER.* Each poem is drawn from a specific chapter found within the Old Testament.

Finola Scott has been published in *The Ofi Press, Obsessed with Pipework , Clear Poetry*, and *Ink, Sweat and Tears* among others. Liz Lochead mentored her on Scotland's Clydebuilt Scheme. She recently read at The Edinburgh Book Festival.

L. Shapley Bassen's *Portrait of a Giant Squid* was the First Place winner in the 2015 *Austin Chronicle* Short Story Contest. Her *What Can the Matter Be?* was the title/featured story in the special KRO Poetics of Science issue, http://www.kenyonreview.org/kr-online-issue/2016-fall/selections/l-shapley-bassen-342846/. She is Fiction Editor for http://www.prickofthespindle.com/ and the author of the novel *Summer of the Long Knives* (Typhoon Media) and *Lives of Crime & Other Stories* (Texture Press) and 2017 publication of a new novella/story collection, *Showfolk & Stories* [Inkception Books]. She was a finalist for the 2011 Flannery O'Connor Award, was a 1st reader for Electric Literature, won the 2009 APP Drama Prize and a Mary Roberts Rinehart Fellowship, and is poetry/fiction reviewer for Brooklyner, The Rumpus, and others. Visit her online at http://www.lsbassen.com/

Sunil Sharma is Mumbai-based senior academic, critic, literary editor and author with 19 published books: Six collections of poetry; two of short fiction; one novel; a critical study of the novel, and, eight joint anthologies on prose, poetry and criticism, and, one joint poetry collection.

He is a recipient of the UK-based Destiny Poets' inaugural Poet of the Year award---2012. His poems were published in the prestigious UN project: *Happiness: The Delight-Tree: An Anthology of Contemporary International Poetry*, in the year 2015. Sunil edits the English section of the monthly bilingual journal Setu published from Pittsburgh, USA: http://www.setumag.com/p/setu-home.html For more details, please visit the blog: http://www.drsunilsharma.blogspot.in/

Jane Simmons is a former teacher/lecturer who has recently completed an MA in Creative Writing at the University of Lincoln. She is now a PhD student at the university of Leicester, where she is working on *The Lyric Self: lyric poetry as a medium for autobiographical life-writing in the work of contemporary British women poets – with a collection of original poems.* Jane has published a collection of poetry, *from darkness into light,* and she is currently working on a novel and a second collection of poetry. She is a member of the Lincoln-based Pimento poets and Outspoken Poets and regularly reads/performs her work in the Lincoln area.

D.J. Tyrer is the person behind *Atlantean Publishing*, was placed second in the 2015 Data Dump Award for Genre Poetry, and has been published in issues of *Amulet, California Quarterly, Carillon, The Dawntreader, Haiku Journal, The Pen*, and *Tigershark*, and online at *Atlas Poetica, Bindweed, Poetry Pacific,* and *Scarlet Leaf Review*, as well as releasing several chapbooks, including the critically acclaimed *Our Story*. DJ Tyrer's website is at http://djtyrer.blogspot.co.uk/ The Atlantean Publishing website is at http://atlanteanpublishing.blogspot.co.uk/

Anne Walsh Donnelly lives in Castleber, Co. Mayo. Her work has been published in *The Irish Times, Crannog* and *Boyne Berries*. One of her poems was highly commended in the OTE New Writer of the Year Award (2017). She was a featured reader at the May 2018 Over The Edge Open Reading. She won the Winter/Spring 2017/18 *Blue Nib* poetry chapbook competition.

www.ingramcontent.com/pod-product-compliance
Lightning Source LLC
Chambersburg PA
CBHW050353100426

42739CB00015BB/3377